ROMAN HISTORY
FROM COINS

Some uses of the Imperial Coinage to the Historian

BY

MICHAEL GRANT
C.B.E., LL.D., Litt.D., F.S.A.

CAMBRIDGE
AT THE UNIVERSITY PRESS
1968

PUBLISHED BY
THE SYNDICS OF THE CAMBRIDGE UNIVERSITY PRESS

Bentley House, 200 Euston Road, London, N.W. 1.
American Branch: 32 East 57th Street, New York, N.Y. 10022

ⓒ CAMBRIDGE UNIVERSITY PRESS 1958

Standard Book Numbers:
521 07348 0 clothbound
521 09549 2 paperback

First published 1958
First paperback
edition 1968

PRINTED IN GREAT BRITAIN BY
HAZELL WATSON AND VINEY LTD
AYLESBURY, BUCKS

CONTENTS

MAP

The Roman Empire and Beyond, in the time of Augustus.

pages 6, 7

THE ROMAN EMPIRE AND BEYOND
IN THE TIME OF AUGUSTUS
31 B.C. – A.D. 14

0   500
English miles

Frontier of Roman Empire — · — · —   Frontier of Parthian Empire · · · · · · · ·
(including dependent States)

paeum
CASUS MTS.
R. Kura
IBERIA
ARMENIA
Artaxata
Carrhae
R. Tigris
R. Euphrates
Europus
Seleucia
Babylon
Basra
PERSIAN GULF
PARTHIAN
EMPIRE
R. Oxus
Tashkurghan
Yarkand
R. Indus
R. Ganges
INDIA
ARABIA
HEJAZ
SABA
Arabia Eudemon
Muziris
COIMB-
ATORE
Arikamedu
C. Comorin
CEYLON
BAY
OF
BENGA
INDIAN
OCEAN

LIST OF PLATES

The Plates are bound together at the end of the book.

FOREWORD

THIS book is intended to show how coins throw light on events of the past. To illustrate this theme I have chosen the coinage of the Roman Empire, which has long been recognized to be of greater historical value than any other of the world's coinages. But I have also included a number of issues of the Greeks, the Byzantines and the neighbours of the Roman Empire—including the British before their annexation. No knowledge of the ancient world, or of coins and their technicalities, has been assumed in the reader, though I hope that those who possess such knowledge will not find the book totally uninteresting.

My aim has been to collect, display and discuss as many significant coins as possible, and yet to ensure that the book should be of relatively low price. Two-hundred and sixty-nine pieces are illustrated in the Plates; of all but twenty, both sides are shown. The majority of Roman emperors and empresses will be found among them. I have tried to make the illustrations as self-contained as possible, so that they can be looked at, and can be enjoyed, without frequent reference to the text; with this intention each Plate bears a brief list of the coins which appear upon it. The commentary, which can obviously make no claim to be comprehensive, is concerned mainly with the earlier and more widely known emperors, but the Plates carry the story onwards to the end of the Western Empire and beyond. It has seemed to me more helpful to arrange the text and Plates by subjects rather than chronologically, though this involves occasional repetition.

The photogravure reproductions have been made by Sun Printers Ltd. For the plaster casts from which they are taken

I want to offer thanks to the British Museum, which has supplied most of them, and also to the authorities of the collections in Berlin (former Kaiser Friedrich Museum), Cambridge, Copenhagen, Glasgow, Milan, Oxford, Paris, Sofia and Stockholm, and to the Rev. H. St J. Hart.

The main part of the book consists of the J. H. Gray Lectures which I delivered at Cambridge for the Faculty of Classics during February 1955, together with portions of talks which I subsequently gave at the Universities of Milan and Genoa. Certain other passages have appeared, in different forms, in *Apollo*, *The Geographical Magazine, London, History Today* and *The Listener*; I owe acknowledgments to their editors. I also wish to thank Mr W. H. Auden and the editors of *The London Magazine* for permission to quote from Mr Auden's poem *Makers of History*, and Mr R. A. G. Carson for assistance with the Plates and their Key. Finally, I am very grateful to the Cambridge University Press for suggesting this book, and for producing it with such kindness and efficiency.

Khartoum and Edinburgh, 1957
Gattaiola, 1968   MICHAEL GRANT

CHAPTER I

HOW RULERS THOUGHT OF THEIR COINS

In order to interpret the significance of ancient coins, we have to forget many features of our modern currency. The passage of two thousand years has changed our ideas about many things, and coinage is one of them. We must begin by forgetting the flatness of modern coins—in both senses of the word—and their sameness over long periods. But if governments had no press and radio (or even postage-stamps) to advertise their achievements and intentions, might they not be forced to advertise them on coinage instead? That is what certain ancient governments did. The only announcements which they could be sure that very many people would see were those on coins. And so they did the best they could with the two small round pieces of space which each coin provided. The results were startling, varied and often beautiful.

We, of course, do not look at our current coinage. Why should we? We know what it looks like already. That is to say, its representations do not often change. Even the details remain the same for dozens of years, and the general appearance of a coin may not be changed for centuries. Besides, the designs are in low relief; they are not in keeping with current artistic movements; they do not challenge the eye. Ancient coin types, on the other hand, did strike the eye. The situation was entirely different. They were noted by thousands of people—sometimes hundreds of thousands. This can be said with confidence, because Greek and Roman governments planned and designed them in such a way that no other conclusion can be drawn.

We need not expect any commentary on this from our literary sources, because, in general, ancient writers say lamentably little about coinage, or indeed about any economic matter (p. 58). But internal evidence provided by the coins themselves is decisive.

Let us consider the Greeks first. Many Greek coins are superb artistic masterpieces, designed by first-rate artists and executed in fine, high relief worthy of a gem (Pl. 1). It is inconceivable that all this trouble should have been incurred by many Greek mints for centuries if nobody were going to notice the result. The rulers of the city-states, the men on whom the mints directly depended, must have believed—and must have continued to believe—that people would notice and appreciate these small masterpieces. Most citizens of Greek communities were more susceptible to works of art than most people in any country today. However, coins did not become beautiful just because of good public taste. Some coins, even of the Periclean Age, are feeble and ugly. But many city-governments deliberately made their coins beautiful. They did so because they thought this was worth while. It was worth while because it was first-rate propaganda. The rulers understood the popular susceptibility to works of art, and concluded that finely executed coin-types would do them good at home and abroad.

But it was not only the city-state Greeks who looked at their current coins. Later, the populations of the Roman Empire did so too. Here the evidence is of a somewhat different character. The first thing that strikes the eye is that usually the heads are startlingly well done at every epoch. The Greeks had latterly produced some fine portraits (Pl. 2, nos. 1 and 2). When the Roman government began to do the same, the first heads were of ancestors (Pl. 2, nos. 3 and 4). But before long Julius Caesar had himself portrayed in his lifetime (Pl. 2, no. 6). Then followed that wonderful series of heads of emperors and empresses, mostly far better executed than portraits on the world's coinage today.

This very high standard is one good reason for saying that Roman coinage, like Greek coinage, was intended to be looked at, and was looked at. We know, independently of the coinage, that successive imperial governments took immense care to tell their massive subject-populations of the ceremonial activities of the emperor's life (Pl. 4); and particular efforts were made to show everyone his features. The autocrats of the twentieth century have likewise made their features well known throughout the areas under their control. Their efforts are accorded a sinister parody in George Orwell's *1984*, which describes the widely distributed portraits of the ruler 'Big Brother' (constructed in such a way that the eyes are always watching you). But no modern dictator distributes his portraits so thoroughly as the Roman 'Fathers of their Country' circulated theirs. It was more important for them than for any modern regime to multiply the portraits of the ruler, for these were respected and venerated by the Romans, for religious reasons, to an altogether special and extra-ordinary extent—perhaps paralleled only in Japan.

So a Roman emperor ensured that there should be a variety of sculptured figures and portrait heads of himself in very many a town and village of the empire. We know of string-ent rules against removing or damaging them. But coins were more portable than busts, and more widely distributed. So, for the dissemination of the ruler's features, the fullest pos-sible use was made of the coinage. Coin-portraits had their share of the veneration accorded to imperial statues; for the coinage was itself under divine patronage (Pl. 5), and was, in due course, even described as 'sacred' (Pl. 5, no. 6).

The Roman authorities, and the artists whom they employed, varied the coin-portraits of an emperor as continually and skilfully as they varied his portrait-busts. He appears in turn as war-lord, priest, far-gazing, semi-divine potentate, unpretentiously bare-headed Italian magistrate. And sometimes his actual features were drastically idealized and rejuvenated. Augustus, particularly, was given this treatment (Pl. 7), and various attempts were made to deal with Nero's heavy features (Pls. 8, 9).

So for hundreds of years the mint poured out a remarkable series of successive imperial faces, intended to impress the personalities and glories of the rulers on their people. Nor did the Roman rulers of the world fail to notice that a coin has two sides. Their subjects were not generally fastidious enough to appreciate great artistry in the reverse type of their coinage. But this deficiency was counterbalanced by their susceptibility to news—and where could they find this news better than on the coinage? So it is with news that its reverses are crammed. And, of course, this news is edifying: it points an imperial moral, and it was selected at a high level.

Sometimes it was presented in the form of a Personification: places are personified, and so are qualities claimed by the imperial rule. In the former category are representations of provinces, such as BRITANNIA (Pl. 19, nos. 3 and 4), ancestors of the type on modern British pennies (p. 55). Nowadays, personifications like this may not convey to us any very vivid message. But in their impact on Roman psychology they appealed directly to strong religious traditions alien from our experience. For instance, the personification of Well-being or Health, SALVS (Pls. 24, no. 7; 27, no. 6), had a host of familiar ancient associations of which governments could make use, associations going far back into the Republic which had portrayed her on its own coinage. Often, too, these personifications carried an implicit, but none the less

14

definite, reference to current policy. LIB*(ertas)* (Pl. 17, no. 2) conveys not only the general associations of, say, the Statue of Liberty; it is also intended to point a contrast between the reigning emperor and an allegedly tyrannical predecessor or rival.

There were stringent conventions and traditions governing the choice of coin-types; and one result of this is that a great many topical references in their designs and inscriptions are indirect, or seem indirect today. For example, there are allusions to anniversaries—allusions often obscure to us but understandable to contemporaries. Very often, we find jubilee coinages recalling the reigning emperor's accession to the throne (Pl. 4, no. 7), and sometimes the accession of great predecessors such as Augustus (Pl. 24, no. 3); whilst anniversaries of the deaths of illustrious ancestors and forerunners were also recorded (Pls. 8, no. 5; 14, no. 8; 24, no. 4). Then, too, the centenaries of antique temples were noted by this ritualistic people, and keen attention was paid to the jubilees of the traditional foundation-date of Rome itself (fixed by Varro at 753 B.C.) (Pl. 25, nos. 1, 5 and 7).[1] For the clearest and most recurrent theme of the coinage is the 'City of Rome' itself, VRBS ROMA; its most ancient and most unmistakable symbols recur again and again (Pl. 3). Indeed, the potency of *Romanità* outlived Rome's eclipse not only as capital of the Roman world—when Constantine replaced it by Constantinople (Pls. 16, no. 8, 19, no. 8); the former Byzantium (Pl. 30, no. 5)—but even as capital of the Western Empire; for its emperors moved, at various times, to Treveri (Trier) (Pl. 17, no. 3), Vienne, Mediolanum (Milan) (Pl. 4, no. 6) and Ravenna (Pls. 17, no. 7; 21, no. 9). But the idea of

[1] The cities of the empire likewise commemorated their anniversaries; for example, Patrae in Greece celebrated the half-centenary of the Roman colony founded there (Pl. 28, no. 4).

Rome lived on, surviving even the shrinking of the frontiers in 476 to exclude, in fact if not in theory, Rome itself (Pl. 3, no. 6). Thereafter the Byzantine Empire continued for a thousand years—lacking Rome (except from the sixth century to the eighth), but still claiming to be Roman (Pl. 26, nos. 9 and 10).

Sometimes, too, there were straightforward allusions to current events. We find references to selected landmarks of the current reign (or an earlier one): for instance important reforms (Pl. 18), or popular building programmes (Pl. 24), or real or pretended victories (Pls. 14–17). Here, and in almost innumerable other cases, we are lucky because we can still see such allusions almost as easily as contemporaries could.

What is most surprising to us is the immense variety of these reverse-designs. In some countries today postage-stamps are often changed, though not in Britain. But how very strange it would seem, in almost any State, if its coinage began to announce the themes of successive new governments with great promptitude, and then altered its message from year to year and month to month as policies shifted.

As evidence for the ancient world, the coins deserve comparison with the ancient writers themselves. W. H. Auden has even suggested that, of the two categories of evidence, the coins are the more reliable:

> Serious historians study coins and weapons,
> Not those reiterations of one self-importance
> By whom they date them,
> Knowing that clerks could soon compose a model
> As manly as any of whom schoolmasters tell
> Their yawning pupils.

It is true, indeed, that the ancient writers are sometimes biased. But they are not always biased *in favour* of the rulers:

for example, our literary record of Tiberius, Nero and Domitian is predominantly hostile, since they are blackened by the historian Tacitus. Here the coins provide us with a counterblast to the writers (see Pls. 8 and 9, for Nero). The emphasis seems strange to readers of the harrowing *Annals*, but it is salutary.

Unfortunately, however, the coins are just as unreliable, just as biased in their different way, as the literary tradition. The heads do not always look just like the men and women whom they represent (though they usually do). The designs and inscriptions do not always indicate what was really happening. Since coins—unlike vases or gems—are public documents, they are as tainted and dangerous as Tacitus (or, for that matter, as pro-government special pleading such as Caesar's *Commentaries*). A few examples of their lies, wishful thoughts and half-truths are collected on Pl. 26.

Yet it is the duty of the historian to weigh up their pro-imperial information against the anti-imperial matter provided by Tacitus. 'I think', wrote Joseph Addison in 1702,[1] 'that your Medallist and Critic are much nearer related than the world imagines.' We need to study the coinage as well as the literature before we can attempt to compile a political history of the Romans.

[1] *Dialogues upon the Usefulness of Ancient Medals* (published 1720).

CHAPTER II

COINS AND PERSONALITIES

I. POSTERITY CONVINCED: AUGUSTUS

WHEN the emperors used their coins for political propaganda, sometimes their versions prevailed over hostile accounts and decisively influenced posterity. But the versions of some other rulers were rejected, and in such cases it is the hostile account that has prevailed throughout the ages. Augustus provides a classic instance of the former situation, Nero of the latter; so I have selected their coinages to show how these two contrasted processes occurred.

The happenings of our own time have thrown into prominence an uncomfortable fact which it is too easy to ignore: that a certain amount of the story has totally and finally disappeared. In the Second World War, General Omar Bradley was worried to think of all the decisions that were being settled over the telephone. The men at the telephone forget and die, and so the historian suffers a defeat. And when rulers actually *want* the historian never to discover what has happened, they often have their way. The survival of Hitler's confidential papers was a lucky chance. In a score of countries at this moment, no such accessible records are likely to save the historian from permanent failure when he tries to reconstruct internal events. And when the events are lost, so are the personalities.

The losses are most serious when a regime is strong and dictatorial and lasts for a long time, so long that none of the few who know survive to tell. For instance, the founder of the long line of Roman emperors, Augustus, lived for most of his seventy-six years in the full glare of publicity—and it still continues, since he was the central figure in a central period of the world's development. Yet he has been described as the man who eludes interpretation more than anyone else in history. It is precisely his greatness, his supremacy, which has made history so difficult. For much business was now kept secret, and this generated false rumours. In the words of the third-century historian Dio Cassius[1]: 'From now on most things that took place began to be kept secret and confidential. Even when public announcements are made, they are distrusted because they cannot be confirmed; for there is a suspicion that all sayings and actions are related to the policy of the rulers and their staffs. As a result there are many rumours about things that have never happened at all—and many things that have certainly happened are quite unknown. . . .' And as Tacitus remarks, such accounts as were written were inconsiderate to future readers, for either they were passionately hostile to the regime, or were passionately servile to it— neither version being true history.

Naturally enough, it was the pro-Augustan interpretation which tended to prevail. The emperor's own official views about his career are seen to this day on the walls of his temple at Ankara, where the carefully phrased Acts of Augustus were incised very shortly after his death by the provincial governor. But we already have a foretaste of this final official version some fifty-seven years earlier, from the first of his great series of coinages—issued only a few months after the murder of Julius Caesar and his own preliminary attempts, at the age of barely twenty, to secure the autocrat's position for himself. Soon the young Octavian (as we are accustomed to call the future Augustus) describes himself as CAESAR, or C(*aius*)

[1] See Note on Ancient and Modern Books, p. 90.

CAESAR, IMP(*erator*) (Pl. 6, no. 2). 'Caesar' refers to Julius Caesar's will, in which Octavian was posthumously adopted as his son, and he was hailed for the first time as 'Imperator' as joint-commander with the two consuls against Antony (January 43 B.C.). With regard to the adoption, modern legal scholars have stressed its extremely rickety and ambiguous juridical bases. But it gained peculiar emotional strength when Caesar was made a 'god' of the Roman State in 42 B.C. (Pl. 6, no. 4).

And then again the conferment of the power (*imperium*), to which the title 'Imperator' on this coin implicitly refers, was continually stressed by Octavian for very many years, and is prominently placed at the beginning of his *Acts* (its centenary and bicentenary were honoured by respectful successors, Pl. 24, no. 3). Yet according to certain ancient writers his initial use of the power was scarcely a matter for such pride, for he allegedly used it to murder both of his joint commanders, the consuls, at the battle of Mutina (Modena). Gossip perhaps, but even gossip is worth putting into the balance against a man's account of himself.

The timely deaths of the consuls induced him to seek the consulship for himself, though he was far below the statutory age. Here again we are able to compare two versions. In Gaul, a few years later, he issued a gold coin bearing his own head, inscribed C(*aius*) CAESAR CO(*n*)S(*ul*) PONT(*ifex*) AVG(*ur*), and on the other side the head of the late Dictator, inscribed C(*aius*) CAESAR DICT(*ator*) PERP(*etuus*) PONT(*ifex*) MAX(*imus*) (Pl. 6, no. 3). Julius Caesar is described as perpetual Dictator and chief priest; Octavian records not only his own membership of two priestly corporations ('Pontifex' and 'Augur') but also, retrospectively, his election by the national Assembly to his first consulship. But we happen to have an ancient, unfavourable account of his election to that consulship. Appian, writing in the second century A.D., tells us that Octavian induced the Senate to support him for the consulship (the Assembly, the elective body, being powerless) by a direct threat of force—exercised through an officer who marched into the Senate and showed the hilt of his sword, crying: 'If *you* won't do it, here's what will!'

Then, says Augustus in his *Acts*, 'the people also made me member of the Triumvirate for setting the State in order. Those who killed my (adoptive) father I drove into exile, punishing their crime by due process of law'. So the coins record with full legality the title of Triumvir (IIIVIR) (Pl. 6, no. 1) which he shared with Antony (Pls. 2, no. 8; 14, no. 5) and Lepidus (Pl. 2, no. 9). The coins also show the beard which Octavian had vowed not to shave until vengeance had been gained (Pl. 6, no. 4)—and finally, after success, they display his Temple of Mars the Avenger (Pl. 7, no. 4). But this 'due process of law' was supplemented, at the very start, by the proscriptions, in which 300 senators (including Cicero and Octavian's guardian) and 2000 other gentry, most of whom had nothing to do with Caesar's murder, were sentenced to death and confiscation. The biographer Suetonius (who as Hadrian's secretary may have had access to certain secret archives) noted initial reluctance by Octavian, but admits that he then carried out the proscriptions more stringently than even his colleagues.

Then, after a series of civil wars culminating in the defeat of Antony at Actium, Augustus became sole ruler. He records that after his victories he spared every citizen who begged for pardon; and that later the Senate presented him with a golden shield commemorating his virtue, piety, justice and clemency. This shield (*clipeus virtutis*), voted by the dependent Senate, was shown to the empire on thousands of coins (Pl. 7, no. 3). But 'let us admit', says the philosopher Seneca, 'that he showed moderation and clemency after the horrors of civil war: yet I do not call sated cruelty clemency'.

'Victory', however, was the principal slogan of Augustus. Coins force it upon the eyes of the vast populations of the Roman world (Pls. 6, nos. 5 and 7; 7, nos. 2 and 4). Other sources (admittedly unreliable) suggest that this martial prowess was not his own. Rumour had it that, when Caesar's assassins were fought at Philippi (42 B.C.), he hid in a marsh; and that during a great sea-battle against Pompey's son he lay asleep and in a stupor while Agrippa (Pl. 7, no. 5) fought and won.

Then Augustus proceeded to claim generosity in his land-settlements for demobilized soldiers; and a huge range of coinages commemorates the allotments they were given in new or expanded citizen 'colonies' (Pl. 6, no. 6). Yet Tacitus tells us how bitterly, just after Augustus' death, such settlers grumbled at the allotments of remote swamp and wild hillside that constituted their 'farms'.

This duality, this marked contrast between the two versions, is everywhere apparent in regard to the new regime. Tacitus knew that Augustus was an autocrat: 'he seduced the army with bonuses, and his cheap food policy was successful. Indeed, he attracted everybody's good will by the enjoyable gift of peace (Pl. 6, no. 8). Then he gradually pushed ahead and absorbed the functions of the Senate, the officials, and even the law. . . .' That last assertion is directly opposed to the emphatic message of Augustus' coins. They, like his *Acts*, incessantly stress the wholly Republican character of the new administration. They stress that he was the Liberator who had saved the lives of citizens (Pls. 6, nos. 8 and 9; 7, no. 1). The *Acts* note that he held no post 'contrary to ancestral tradition'; that he had 'transferred the State from his own control to the free will of the Senate and Roman People'—and to those traditional components of the Roman State, the s.p.q.r., there are many honorific references on the coins (Pl. 7, nos. 1 and 3).

Such then are the direct contradictions that confront us. But very often our attempt to reach the truth is faced with an even worse difficulty. So far, I have selected some of the relatively few happenings where there *is* a corrective to the coins and to the *Acts* (even if it is only gossip). Usually, however, there is no such corrective, for Augustus was supreme for a very long time. And then we have to look at the messages on his coins with a carefully sceptical eye. Yet, even when we have no check on them, they are not merely a smoke-screen; their types and inscriptions are of great positive significance. For they reveal many facts concerning the psychology of the Romans for whom they were designed. Once Augustus has become supreme ruler, their appeal is deliberately emotional, far from realities. They do not admit that Augustus controlled most of the army and was therefore an autocrat. Their appeal is to titles with an emotional content—*Son of a God, Chief Priest, Father of the Country* (Pl. 7, no. 7). Through these titles and these coins Augustus worked on the sentimental, traditional, antiquarian feelings of his peoples, and particularly of the Italians, who formed the nucleus of the empire and its armies.

He made use of certain curious, ingrained Roman and Italian social ideas which seem to us almost feudal in character; and by these he was able to bind almost everyone in awe and loyalty to himself. According to the Roman way of thinking there were singularly strong bonds between powerful people and those hosts of poorer, weaker men called their 'clients'. These bonds imposed binding, hereditary sanctions. Augustus, with all the prestige of his title as Caesar's heir and of his own highly successful record, exploited these ideas—

23

with a weighty force behind him, but this was kept well in the background.

At critical stages, too, he invited and organized 'spontaneous' oaths of loyalty. By such means he attached to himself, in a potent but non-legal or supra-legal way, the numerous officials and peoples of the empire. And having secured their allegiance he was in a position to exert his authority more widely, by the mere exercise of his apparently informal but heavily prestige-laden advice, without having to affirm that he was acting in accordance with any legally conferred power. Every coin brings forward some aspect, or several aspects, of this non-legal, supra-legal glamour of the universal Patron, Father and Refounder.

The Romans were more accustomed than we are to respected figures exerting authority with a purely moral or social justification. Augustus had acquired all the needful qualifications and so he was able, by such informal or indirect means, to ensure that action of many kinds was taken. For example, the brass and copper coinages at Rome which bear the Senate's signature, s(*enatus*) c(*onsulto*) (Pl. 7, no. 1), were probably initiated by a motion incorporating his 'advice' to the Senate. This Republican façade corresponded with a constitutional and psychological necessity. For Roman public opinion was highly sensitive on formal points like this. It was therefore essential that the Roman constitution should still *look* as Republican as possible. By the judicious use of informal advice to subservient officials, Augustus could deal with many matters without having to brandish openly his real autocratic power; and that is the spirit in which the coinage is designed. Thus, if he wanted to speak of his authority in any but purely emotional terms, he stressed the bases not of his overwhelming *power* but of his modest, reassuring constitutional *powers*. Modern students of Augustus have become accustomed to draw a pretty firm distinction between the *constitution* of the Augustan State on the one hand—good, sound stuff—and wicked un-British propaganda on the other. But perhaps the distinction ought to be blurred. If it was in the interests of Augustus' propaganda that such-and-such a feature should, or should not, be part of the constitution, was it really so hard for him (through acquiescent lawyers, who were not lacking) to insert that feature, or leave it out?

Good window-dressing is planned for some particular section or sections of the public, and so presumably were the designs of this coinage. Certain of them spoke for themselves; even illiterates could see the significance of a figure of Victory. According to one view, the upper classes were the target for the refinements of publicity—'or rather, it should be said, they gradually formulated the reasons and excuses for accepting the new order of things'.[1] Another suggestion is that the people for whom the most elaborate pretences were necessary were the great old-fashioned middle-class of Italy[2], rather as the Tudor monarchy made its appeal to the rising middle-class of England.

But national propaganda as extensive and careful as that of Augustus was capable of angling at more than one class, however important. We can sometimes tell nowadays whether a coinage was only a small, semi-private issue or one of portentous dimensions intended to reach a million eyes. And we can also tell where it circulated: for instance, Pl. 6, no. 2 shows a plain western head of Augustus, and Pl. 6, no. 10 a portrait designed for regions more familiar with Hellenistic monarchy. But that is only one simple example of a phenomenon as complicated as the multiple Roman Empire itself. A task which now lies before numismatists is to dis-

[1] Professor Sir Ronald Syme.   [2] Professor A. H. M. Jones.

entangle and distinguish those particular themes of publicity which were intended chiefly for this or that particular stratum or interest. The results, deduced from the coinage, will at least be based on solid, contemporary objects, designs and words; and that cannot be said of most other categories of evidence.

And yet the only reason why we have the coins at all is because Augustus himself had them made. The initiative in issuing coinage came from the emperor; and either he or one of his advisers chose the designs, or at least gave general directions concerning them. What Augustus shows the world is his soft velvet glove. For our knowledge of the iron hand underneath we have to be content with gossip reported by men writing a century, or even two centuries, later. From *his* Chancery we have had no lucky discoveries of secret, tell-tale records correcting the coins by a less attractive picture of events. So Hitler, with his elaborate confidential records which failed to remain confidential, had a good deal to learn from Augustus.

For historians, politicians and philosophers, Augustus is the classic illustration of a universal problem: the problem of the man of action who intended to impose his own account on posterity, and whose efforts to do so have been successful.

2. POSTERITY UNCONVINCED: NERO

The propaganda of Nero, the last emperor of Augustus' dynasty, was as vigorous as that of Augustus. But, unlike his, it has failed to convince posterity; and the two men may be taken as typical of the two contrasted sorts of fate which propaganda may suffer.

Every epoch has had its say about Nero. The crescendo of measured denunciation was reached in the nineteenth century. De Quincey saw in Nero 'the first in that long line of monsters who . . . under the title of Caesars dishonoured human-ity'. To the historian Merivale, Nero was 'the despot released from all fear of God and overwhelmed at the same time with the fear of man . . who has no equal in history, to whom no analogy may be found save in the pathological annals of the scaffold'. Merivale called him 'vulgar, timid and sanguinary' —an adequate description, for although Nero possessed artistic and imaginative qualities, few rulers have been so thoroughly criminal and fatuous.

These qualities are profusely illustrated in the surviving ancient accounts of his reign. Though Tacitus, Suetonius and Dio Cassius wrote a long time after his death, all three were strongly influenced by the hatred felt for Nero, during his lifetime, by highly placed Romans. These writers do not suffer from lack of abusive material. When Tacitus had denigrated an earlier emperor, Tiberius (Pl. 32, no. 4), the in-tractability of his subject-matter—for Tiberius was glum but not unspeakable—had caused him to adopt, for greater con-viction, a lurid, hinting, smearing style. His account of Nero, whose deplorable actions speak for themselves, can afford to be more straightforward.

But the mighty imperial machine had reached a high pitch of efficiency and was affected only slowly by evil or idiocy at the centre. Indeed, a bad emperor might have no adverse effect whatever on the lives of millions of his subjects. They might benefit from what benefits were available without suffering from shocks inflicted on prominent metropolitan Romans and reflected by their historians. This had apparently happened under that earlier freak Caligula (Pls. 28, no. 3; 30, no. 2). It is necessary to consider whether the same does not apply to Nero.

We shall not be in a position to discount the lies and half-truths of the historians until we have had a look at Nero's own lies and half-truths: at the statements which he and his government judged it possible and desirable to make in favour of their policies. Nero's case is very carefully put forward on his coins. We can seldom be sure whether a Roman emperor chose his own designs personally (p. 26). But Nero probably did. For he was an artist; and his coinage displays marked artistic improvement. It becomes more beautiful than any other Roman series—and perhaps finer than coinage has ever been since.

This aesthetic climax was not attained immediately after Nero's accession (A.D. 54). But even the earliest coinages served their political purpose, for they said and implied a good deal about his government's point of view. Pl. 8, no. 1 shows on one side the seventeen-year-old Nero and his domineering mother Agrippina (cf. Pl. 10, no. 3)—already, in a few months, reduced from first to second place. On the reverse, in ceremonial chariot, is Augustus (whom Nero persistently pretended to imitate) with Nero's immediate predecessor Claudius (whom he officially 'deified', joking that mushrooms—with which Agrippina had poisoned him —were 'the food of the gods'). The large letters EX S(*enatus*) C(*onsulto*), 'from a decree of the Senate', remind us of Nero's initial attention to that body, which he soon, however, came to detest. Cautious, respectable continuity is the keynote of these designs; and probably they circulated more widely than any disparaging rumours.

Six years later a new programme was selected for the coinage. One of the new 'types' is a warrior (Pl. 8, no. 2). He represents the antique, traditional quality of the Roman Republic, martial valour and endurance: *Virtus*. This new representation is exceedingly at variance with our literary record of Nero, the pro-Greek monarch who received senators in a short, flowered tunic and muslin scarf (and shocked one writer, Dio Cassius, by using bath-salts). In the previous year, too, he had murdered his mother, Agrippina: a horrible tale, far removed from good old Roman *Virtus*. (Jewish morality, expressing itself in 'Sibylline Oracles', was especially shocked.)

> O heart, lose not thy nature; let not ever
> The soul of Nero enter this firm bosom:
> Let me be cruel, not unnatural.

But Hamlet does not add that Nero, despite his own nervousness—and isolated hostile slogans and acts of sabotage—was enthusiastically acclaimed when, after the deed, he returned to Rome. Many of the flatterers were evidently less shocked than relieved to be rid of a terribly dangerous woman. Tacitus faithfully records the excellent reception given him.

In any case, the introduction of old Roman *Virtus* soon after such an event is not so startling and macabre as it looks. For in Britain, fighting under Nero's supreme command shortly before these coins were issued, Paulinus had won a spectacular victory by annihilating the Druid human sacrificers and their sanguinary females on Mona (Anglesey). Nero, though highly unwarlike by temperament, came from army stock of which much was expected, and was called 'Caesar' like other emperors. All the more need for a justificatory martial success under his auspices, and here it was (though the fruits of victory were soon lost owing to the revolt of Boudicca—'Boadicea'). So in A.D. 60 and the following years Romans were encouraged to think less of matricide and Greek acting than of their emperor's victorious new manhood. A contemporary issue strikes the same note by displaying, in military costume, Roma herself; and the same theme, in improved form, recurs throughout the reign (Pl. 8, no. 3).

Four years after the first 'Roma' issues, Nero began his unprecedentedly magnificent series of brass and copper coinages. It gives a vigorous impression of the ruler himself, unduly bloated for his twenty-six years (Pls. 8, 9). (We are told that, although Nero was not ill-favoured, his complexion and eyes were unattractive, and his paunch as fat as his neck, but his legs much too thin; his health, despite excesses, was good.) Pl. 8, no. 4 offers a curious commentary on the theme of Roma. For her 'protectors', and the protectors of its emperor who owed them his throne and paid them for it, were the Praetorian Guardsmen; and here, for publicity purposes (scarcely a year before their officers plotted against him), is Nero at their manoeuvres (DECVRSIO). This is a tactful reference to the Guard, which was otherwise, in publicity, almost unmentionable owing to its incompatibility with the Republican façade. Its successive commanders were Nero's counsellors: first Burrus, until he died in questionable circumstances; then Tigellinus, a vicious ex-breeder of race-horses. Tigellinus was in power, joint-commander of the Guard with an ineffective colleague, when this coin was struck.

Nero shared his love of horses; he loved riding and driving chariots, and always had. As a boy, he had been forbidden even to mention the word Circus. As emperor, he defended chariot-racing as royal, ancient and sanctified by religion and poetry. (When an official, irritated by the *prima donna* behaviour of charioteers, tried to replace horses by dogs, Nero intervened.) After he had been emperor for five years (A.D. 59), his advisers had reluctantly agreed to his driving, in person, in the new Vatican Circus—before a *private* audience; but despite senatorial alarm the public soon secured admission, and enjoyed the unique spectacle immensely. Nero's 'horsiness' was so popular that he wore his front hair 'set' and 'crimped' in steps, like a charioteer's; and that is actually how these coins show it. But it was imprudent of him to spend so much of his last two years (A.D. 66–68) chariot-driving in Greece. In the Olympic Games he fell and did not complete the course, but the judges politely proclaimed him the winner (thus earning a large subsidy). Back in Rome he hung some of his trophies round his bedroom, and gave a public exhibition comprising no less than 1,808 of them. Pl. 8, no. 4 shows how the coins deal with this embarrassing imperial taste. Discreetly and delicately, they allude to its utility for Roman, warlike purposes.

An approximately contemporary coin shows Apollo the lyre-player (Pl. 9, no. 1). This refers to an even more passionate taste of Nero's which offended prominent Romans still more deeply, without stimulating—in the West at least—any counterblast of popular enthusiasm. This was his devotion to the theatre. He loved acting, and especially singing. Often what he sang was poetry composed by himself; and he played the lyre while he sang. He practised fanatically, dieting and taking laxatives and lying on his back with heavy sheets of lead across his torso. The quality of his voice and his poetry is variously reported; probably neither was bad. His husky tones were best adapted to melodramatic parts. The future emperor Vespasian hazardously slept while Nero performed, but other generals and senators felt all too wakeful when they saw their emperor acting as a beggar, runaway slave, lunatic and pregnant woman. A loyal but uncultured soldier saw him rattling his chains on the stage, and leapt up to take them off. 'What is the emperor doing?' went a joke about another role; 'is he having a baby?'

His advisers had hoped that if Nero were allowed to drive chariots he might forget his ambition to act on the public stage. But they were wrong. The very year of these coins, when Burrus was dead and Seneca not long for this world, witnessed his début. Hellenic Naples was chosen for it. Then he 'starred' on the professional stage of Rome itself. Naturally there is a rich crop of stories—about how one had to feign dead to get out of the theatre, how Nero obeyed theatrical etiquette so strongly that he would not even spit, and so on. 'What a loss to the profession!' was what he meant to convey in those untranslatable last words of his life (*qualis artifex pereo*). It is only too painfully probable that this author of an epic on the Fall of Troy sang it, and *fiddled while Rome burnt*; the appropriately lurid background must have been irresistible.

All writers agree that his performances on the professional stage were unspeakably shocking to leading Romans—as shocking, perhaps, as his murders, and much more shocking than his immoralities. It is therefore curious and interesting to see from Pl. 9, no. 1 that the usually conservative and discreet coinage saw fit to acquaint the world with this imperial taste. Perhaps it was felt that something had to be said. So it was said with a masterly mixture of cunning and boldness. For Apollo the lyre-player had appeared just once before—on the much less well-executed coinage of that most 'respectable' of all personages, Nero's ancestor the divine Augustus (Pl. 7, no. 6). Augustus had conveyed, by this design, his thanks to his patron Apollo for the decisive sea victory over Antony at Actium; and statues of Apollo in the same guise had been prominent in contemporary buildings. Augustus, imply Nero's coins, had favoured Greek learning and art (over which Apollo presided); so does Nero—and the obvious differences are ignored. To say, with Suetonius, that Nero was actually *identified* with Apollo on these coins is to go further than official terminology permits—though it was no doubt widely said by contemporaries, and his too-long back hair on these coins is deliberately Apolline. But the reverse type cannot fairly be called anything more than Augustan;

and, when Nero re-entered the capital after his Greek 'victories', he chose to ride in Augustus' triumphal chariot.

So here is that favourite 'propaganda-line' of almost all emperors—the similarity of their conduct to that of the deified Augustus. Quite undisturbed by a fantastic widening of the gap between Nero's behaviour and that of his cold, cautious forebear, his government persists with the theme. Pl. 8, nos. 5 and 6 show what could be made of it. Both these designs—Victory carrying a shield inscribed s.p.q.r. and Vesta's revered temple—were intimately and inseparably associated with the memory of Augustus: these two representations had appeared only once before, and that had been in his posthumous honour (Pl. 7, nos. 8 and 9). They had appeared simultaneously on that occasion, and now—to confirm that the coincidence is not fortuitous—they reappear simultaneously under Nero; and their reappearance coincides with the half-century of Augustus' death. But on Roman coins antiquarianism is habitually blended with topicality, and here too there is a topical allusion: for in the same year A.D. 64 Vesta's shrine was destroyed in the Fire, and Nero, who was affected by the cult (he had recently felt faint in the temple), rebuilt it. The shield carried by Victory on the prototypes of Pl. 8, no. 5 had been a golden shield dedicated to Augustus by the Senate and Roman People (s.p.q.r.) in recognition of his classic, cardinal virtues (Pl. 7, no. 3); and now it refers to Nero's claim that these same virtues are incarnated in his own regime and confer on him that half-magical property of Victoriousness.

It is usually forgotten that Nero's military and foreign policy achieved remarkable successes. This year A.D. 64, in particular, was the climax of a brilliant period. Even Tacitus concedes that *peace had never been so profound*. This is only a grudging aside from his horror-stories, but Nero, unlike his enemies, proclaimed the fact widely. Pl. 8, no. 7 displays a proud, antique formula referring to the ceremonial closure of the temple of Janus on the rare occasions when Rome was wholly at peace—'The Peace of the Roman People having been won on land and sea, he closed Janus'—and the shrine is shown. Augustus had closed it three times, but in all the centuries preceding him only two similar occasions were known. On these coins of *c.* A.D. 64 Nero announces a forthcoming closure, because through his general Corbulo—by negotiation (p. 47) —he had tackled and solved the question of Armenia, interminably disputed between Rome and Parthia. Finally, in A.D. 66, the ceremony took place; perhaps the date had been postponed for the tercentenary of the first recorded closure (235 B.C.). Romans saw the unprecedented sight of Tiridates, brother of the King of Parthia, waiving all the taboos of his Zoroastrian faith by officially visiting Rome itself to do homage to Nero—who fortified him with an immense daily allowance— and to receive the diadem of Armenia from him.

'Nero's solution,' said M. P. Charlesworth, 'was ... diplomatically superb; for fifty years there was peace.' Indeed peace is much celebrated by Neronian poets—*candida Pax*, *perpetua Pax*, the pastoral Calpurnius Siculus calls it; and certain coins, with their usual topical but backward-looking tact, display an Altar of Peace (ARA PACIS) imitated from, if not identical with, Augustus' famous altar of the same name at Rome. Another more difficult inscription, 'The Security of the Augustus' (SECVRITAS AVGVSTI) (Pl. 8, no. 8) may conceivably (though further research seems necessary) mean 'The Security conferred by (Nero) Augustus'.

If so, it is somewhat parallel to the inscription on Pl. 9, no. 3, with its much admired composition of ANNONA AVGVSTI, the personification of 'the Corn-Supply provided by the Augustus', and CERES, goddess of the crops. It was the

34

emperor's responsibility to feed Rome, to see that the corn-ships reached its harbours (as they had often failed to do unless he intervened), and to organize lavish distributions of free or cheap grain. Greek philosophical theories, to which Roman coin-propaganda often subscribed (and Nero had imbibed them from Seneca), encouraged the proclamation of *service* by the ruler to his people. In practical terms, Romans regarded the emperor's chief function as the provision of food (cf. Pl. 20, nos. 2 and 4). On this coin Nero celebrates his success. He was determined to be generous and popular, whatever the cost, and Tacitus—writing of this year A.D. 64 —is bound to admit that the people of the capital found his presence so beneficial that they hated the idea of his going on a foreign tour; so he postponed it.

But in this same year came the Great Fire, with its terrible rumours of imperial incendiarism. The rumours were certainly untrue—as were the similar charges in 1666 against James Duke of York, who, like Nero, tried to put the fire out. But Nero felt it would be desirable to find scapegoats; and he judged the unpopular Christians to be suitable for this purpose. Very soon, however, irritation was caused by his vast new 'Golden House'. The government was again able to tell a very different story. Not only were antique shrines piously and expensively restored (cf. Pl. 8, no. 6), but an appeal could also again be made to the people's appetites: Pl. 9, no. 4 shows the commodious Provision-Market—MAC(*ellum*) AVG(*usti*)—completed by Nero five years earlier, and no doubt one of the first buildings to be rebuilt after the Fire. He also reminded them that supplies were improved by the great new harbour he had opened at Ostia (p. 52; Pl. 9, no. 2). The harbour had been constructed by Claudius; but even if only Nero's own building activities are considered, the official case in his favour is a fair one. A famous emperor,

Trajan, referred eulogistically to the construction programme of Nero's 'five years'—by which he probably meant his *last* five years (A.D. 64–68). As the epigrammatist Martial put it:

> What is worse than Nero?
> What is better than Nero's Baths?

After the fire of A.D. 64, Rome was replanned very wisely. Yet even this wise expenditure, added to the cost of warfare and ingratiating generosity, amounted to ruinous sums. So did Nero's fantastic personal extravagance. Despite his physical training, he spent much of most days having dinner; perhaps this helped him to appreciate the people's desire for food.

Yet the government, all the time, had its own point of view and had many people on its side. It is true that when the final crisis came in A.D. 68—starting with the obscure revolt of Vindex in Gaul, which failed but soon brought Galba (Pl. 14, no. 10) to the throne from Spain—the debit side of Nero's reputation proved, in terms of power, to exceed the credit side. But it might not have been so, if he had not feebly collapsed long before all was lost. And it had not been so for most of his fourteen years on the throne: these coins, with their persuasive arguments and gigantic circulation, suggest why.

Moreover, his posthumous reputation was sensational. As a philosopher of the next century, Dio Chrysostom, observed: 'Still, even now, all men long for Nero to be alive—and most men actually believe to this day that he is living.' So Nero's desire for posthumous fame was gratified. Pseudo-Neros proliferated and won many followers—especially in the East, and among the admiring Parthians. And while no holds are barred in Christian tradition, bronze tokens relating to the Roman Games showed Nero's head more than three hundred years after his death (Pl. 9, no. 6). Here, for a pagan populace in an officially Christian Rome, is Nero patron of the Circus. Memories of Nero's benefactions must have been remarkably tenacious.

Equally remarkable were early obituary tributes only a few months after his death. Otho had lost his wife Poppaea (Pl. 10, no. 5) to Nero. In order to marry her, Nero had sent Otho away to govern Lusitania (Portugal), and had divorced and murdered, in particularly revolting circumstances, his own first wife Octavia (Pl. 10, no. 4). There were rumours that Otho encouraged Nero's devotion to Poppaea. Nevertheless, when he became emperor (Pl. 26, no. 1), Otho, as well as wearing a wig imitating Nero's hair-style, found it politically advisable to honour his memory. And then again, immediately afterwards —still in A.D. 69, the 'Year of the Four Emperors'—Vitellius (Pl. 14, no. 11) would say at his gluttonous dinner-parties *Now sing us one of the Master's songs*. The Master was Nero; nothing would have pleased him more.

Yet Nero's self-defence on his coins has, on the whole, failed to convince the world. He had killed too many senators to please the ancient historians, who mostly had senatorial sympathies; and he had killed too many Christians, and led too outrageous a private life, to win the favour of a Christian posterity.

3. IMPERIAL WOMEN ON COINS

Pls. 10–13 show something of the extraordinary portrait gallery of women on the Roman coinage. Feminine portraits on our own coinage are relatively unusual; throughout our history, scarcely a dozen women have been thus represented. On the coins of the Greek cities and the Roman Empire, however, innumerable women were depicted. In Greece many of them posed as models for the goddesses who occupied the obverses of coins (Pl. 1, nos. 4 and 7). Later, in the great Hellenistic monarchies which were carved out of Alexander's conquests, they appeared as royal consorts and even as rulers.

The last of these monarchies to hold out against Rome was Egypt; and the last of its rulers was Cleopatra (Pl. 10, no. 1). Her lightly waved hair, with its single chignon, seems to suggest that Cleopatra, like a goddess, did not need too complex a coiffure. But she wears the diadem which, according to Roman propagandists, she wished to impose on Italy. This silver coin was issued in her honour by a Graeco-Jewish city on her frontiers—Ascalon. She was overlord of Ascalon, as of much else in the Levant, because of her influence on Antony.

Can we see anything here of 'the charm and enchantment of her passing beauty and grace'? Not, perhaps, very much, though her somewhat pensive expression is interesting—if not due to wear of the coin. But Cleopatra lived at the turning of the ways. Hellenistic coin-portraiture was long past its best; the series of Roman female coin-portraits was just about to begin.

This series came into being because the Roman State unlike ours—was accustomed to portray on its coins not only the sovereign but his wife, and very often also his female relatives, alive and dead. Many of them were powerful and formidable. Though women could not hold office, they were traditionally influential, and the early empire produced some terrifying autocrats and termagants.

Pl. 10, no. 2 hints at the strong will of the elder Agrippina, wife of the popular Germanicus. Granddaughter of Augustus, grandmother of Nero, both relationships become apparent in the career of this frustrated widow, and both may perhaps be seen in her posthumous portrait. Hair fashions have changed since Cleopatra's chignon. Agrippina wears a tightly plaited queue, which is folded back and bound at the nape of her neck with a ribbon. She also wears elaborate side-ringlets which (as statues show) were puffed out—a Greek style adopted, some have said, because the first emperors favoured archaic tastes. But one of Agrippina's curls escapes to fall spirally beneath her ear, a conceit which she and her contemporaries (some of whom multiplied the wayward lock) handed on to the Italian ladies commemorated on fifteenth-century medallions. When this portrait of Agrippina was designed, there was already a splendid tradition of realistic, idealistic or pathetic Italian portrait busts. Here are no signs of Hellenistic pathos. Indeed, Agrippina looks very Roman. Yet in technique the debt to Greece was immense, and engravers were still mostly Greek. The portrait seems Roman not because its artist was Roman, but because its subject was Roman.

Agrippina's origins were mixed, but she was brought up in elevated circles and she looks aristocratic. The next (Flavian) dynasty was bourgeois in origin, but Pl. 11, no. 1 shows how its ladies adopted smart hair-styles with which the middle-class could not compete. Here Julia, the daughter of Titus, wears a large, no doubt artificial, fringe of tightly clustering curls known as the 'honeycomb' coiffure; it is described for us by poets. Julia has returned to the chignon, drawn tight by a ribbon and worn higher than Cleopatra's. She has abandoned the rather austere queue; when she was older she revived it, in a different form (Pl. 11, no. 2). Her aunt Domitia, the wife of Domitian, displays her own version of both styles (Pl. 10, nos. 6 and 7). Coins and portrait-busts of this date achieve a new, fluid individualism—they present their subject as a personality with a social background. But then, in the reign of the conqueror Trajan, the chief women at court were staid and elderly. This gave a good opportunity to artists who, though mainly Greek themselves, had long catered for the biographical tastes of Romans by depicting old people realistically. Old women were no longer idealized; and it had become fashionable to stress character in wives.

Plotina (Pl. 11, no. 5), shown with her late husband Trajan, is straightforward, dignified, correct and unpretentious—far removed from one lively octogenarian contemporary who kept a troupe of private actors. Yet, while reverting to the plaited queue of the earlier empire, Plotina does not disdain to wear a high diadem and equally lofty pompadour, in front of which (as statues indicate more clearly) a metal band joined to the diadem encircled the brow. Other ladies of this respectable court favoured still greater elaboration. One of them is Trajan's sister Marciana (Pl. 11, no. 3), portrayed opposite the imperial eagle which had recently carried her to heaven. The even more surprising pompadour of her daughter Matidia (Pl. 11, no. 4) seems to be made of some solid material, so regular and rigidly coiled are her artificial locks, rising to a lofty protuberance in the centre of the brow. Behind, the queue is abandoned, the plaits being tightly gathered up to leave the nape shorn and hairless.

Some have seen in the portrait-busts of these women a new, anxious hardness of expression, perhaps due in part to Trajan's frequent warfare. At any rate, they look capable. And they faced a crisis on which the peace of the world depended. Plotina was very fond of the brilliant Hadrian, her relative by marriage, and wanted him to succeed to the throne. But he still had not been adopted or granted the usual preliminary share in the imperial power when Trajan, weakened by his unremitting exertions in the East, sickened with dropsy. Leaving Hadrian behind to govern Syria and its army, he turned westwards, but became more gravely ill and, as he traversed the south coast of Asia Minor, died at Selinus in Cilicia. The army in Syria declared Hadrian emperor, and Rome—some time later—was told that Trajan, on his death-bed, had adopted him (Pl. 26, no. 3). There were (and are) grave, insoluble doubts whether this was true. One of the few who might have known, Trajan's personal servant, died suddenly about two days after his master. The secret remained locked in the bosoms of one man—the Commander of the Guard—and two women: Plotina and Matidia. Imperial women needed cool judgment and iron nerves.

Beauty returned in the households of the two enlightened emperors Antoninus Pius and Marcus Aurelius. Their wives—mother and daughter—were both called Faustina. Both were loaded with honours by their husbands. Both too (perhaps because their husbands exaggerated these attentions) were savagely attacked by contemporary gossip. The mother (Pl. 11, no. 7), who was to inspire Renaissance medallists, evidently wound her braided queues round her head three or even four times. The daughter, as a young bride, wears her hair care-fully waved in front and, at the back, gathered into a plaited 'coronet' imitated by ladies of Napoleon's First Empire (Pl. 11, nos. 8 and 9). These braids were probably kept in place by sewing (as they were in the nineteenth century); and pre-sumably the ladies slept in their hair.

In spite of her lively temperament, the younger Faustina's philosopher husband was devoted to her. He allowed her to be called 'Mother of the Camp' and, when she died in a remote corner of the empire, mourned her sincerely. In prac-tice, evidently, his Stoicism did not oblige him to agree with that earlier Roman citizen Paul of Tarsus (brought up in the same creed) that women should 'adorn themselves . . with shamefacedness and sobriety, not with braided hair'. The

41

younger Faustina experimented in hair-styles. Sometimes the coinage shows a wave of curls; often they are symmetrically arranged (Pl. 21, no. 1), occasionally they are massed in a ridge—perhaps kept in place by some glutinous material. At other times Faustina favoured classic simplicity.

Ovid had long since commented, in his *Art of Love*, on the diversity of female coiffures. Indeed, portrait-busts are sometimes found to possess detachable marble wigs which could be replaced as fashions altered. Because of such changes in ancient coiffures, the dated coins on which they appear are of the greatest assistance in dating female portrait-statues showing comparable styles; even away from Rome, the centre of fashion, the time-lags among upper-class ladies were not very long.

After the Antonines, in the dynasty of the Severi, a woman reached a new degree of eminence almost amounting to co-rulership of the empire. This was Julia Domna (Pl. 12, no. 3). In her day the throne was habitually occupied by men who were not Italians. Her husband, Septimius Severus, who used drastic means to protect the Roman world against worsening external threats, came from Lepcis Magna (Tripolitania). His wife was Syrian. She is described as artful, malicious, immoral; the wife of a Scottish chieftain is said to have snubbed her for strictures on Caledonian laxity. But Julia Domna was a shrewd judge of events, and an intellectual deeply interested in the eastern religious movements that now pervaded Roman thought (Pl. 21). Round her were men like Philostratus (biographer of the miracle-working mystic Apollonius of Tyana) and Galen, father of western medicine.

Julia Domna is credited by some with the reintroduction of the oriental wig. At all events, strange coiffures were back again. Like the vigorously waved Didia Clara (Pl. 12, no. 2)—daughter of the transient emperor Didius Julianus—Julia

Domna started her imperial life with a large bun or *tourteau*. Then she adopted a queue tucked into a much smaller bun. Next, after the death of her husband at Eboracum (York), when she became (in early middle age) virtually regent in domestic affairs for her unbalanced monster of a son Caracalla, she proceeded to the novel coiffure shown on Pl. 12, no. 3. The bun has become a mere knot. Beneath a diadem resembling an oriental crescent, the curled braids are not caught up, but hang like the lappets of a helmet, covering all but the front of her face—a curious fashion which was to return, for men as well as women, in the Renaissance. Julia Domna's face is expressive. Feminine psychology was in fashion; and the recently instituted custom of dotting the eye made for greater vividness. This occurs on coins as well as busts, though it does not come out very clearly in a photograph.

Julia Domna died a few months after Caracalla was assassinated. But within a year her equally brilliant sister Julia Maesa (Pl. 12, no. 4) had successfully turned king-maker, placing on the throne her fourteen-year-old grandson Elagabalus, priest of an orgiastic cult in Syria (p. 56; Pl. 21, no. 4): his mother and successive wives are also excellently portrayed on coins (Pl. 12, nos. 5–8). Julia Maesa was perhaps more coldly astute than her sister Domna. But Elagabalus, with his fantastic and fanatical excesses, proved an irremediable embarrassment. Realizing this, Julia Maesa gradually brought forward his respectable young cousin, Severus Alexander. Before long the priest-emperor and his mother were murdered, and Severus Alexander came to the throne. His mother Julia Mamaea (Pl. 13, no. 1) guided his footsteps, and his grandmother Julia Maesa died in peace.

These third-century heads remind us that amid the growing chaos portraiture, far from deteriorating, rose to new heights of expressiveness; and there were further fine female portraits to come (e.g. Pl. 13, nos. 3, 6, and 10). Here I have mentioned a small, symbolic selection from an immense and varied range of portraits. Even today, authentic coins portraying with great skill some of these beautiful or formidable personages can be acquired for a few shillings.

CHAPTER III

THE EMPIRE ON ITS COINAGE

I. WAR

NOT only the rulers and their wives, but the empire itself, in all its vicissitudes, is mirrored on the designs of Roman coinage. Time after time it throws light on the relation of Rome to the territories which it governed. Often the coins convey messages or implications which confirm or supplement, or even contradict, what the ancient writers tell us. One such series of allusions reflects the triumphs and aspirations of the Roman rulers in their wars. This is an abundant, dominant theme in Rome's history and propaganda: the defeat, conquest and suppression of hostile or recalcitrant countries.

The most elementary and conventional device of conquest is the trophy. It appears, for example, on a silver *denarius* of Julius Caesar (Pl. 14, no. 2), after he had conquered northern and central Gaul (and finally Vercingetorix, hero of the Resistance) with that well-known brutality which awakens our guilt-complexes today. Probably this coin of military design was issued in Gaul itself, in payment of troops whom he was about to lead across the Rubicon against Pompey on 10 January, 49 B.C.

After that mighty upheaval, the murder of Caesar caused another. The Roman world was torn between his temporarily united heirs (Pls. 2, no. 8; 6, no. 2) and his assassins (Pls. 2, no. 7; 14, no. 3). Anarchy produced semi-independent *condottieri*. One of them was the admiral Ahenobarbus (Pl. 2, no. 10). Another, Quintus Labienus (Pl. 14, no. 4), was something of a freak. He was not merely a quasi-independent war-lord; he was in the employment of the national enemy King Orodes II of Parthia, beyond the Euphrates (Pl. 32, no. 10). When Caesar's assassins met their end at Philippi in 42 B.C., Labienus fled to Parthia.

It was only eleven years since Parthia had inflicted an unforgettable defeat on Rome at Carrhae (Haran) in Meso-potamia. The victory was owed to Parthia's famous light cavalry, of which Labienus insultingly shows a horse on this coin. Quintus Labienus was the son of a good Roman general and was a good general himself. Based on Cilicia (south-east Asia Minor)—where these coins were perhaps minted—he was not suppressed until he had overrun the whole peninsula, right to its western areas; and with the prosperity of that wealthy, Hellenized country the credit of the Roman money-market was intimately linked. The hostility of Quintus Labienus to Rome is emphasized by his self-description as PARTHICVS—not 'conqueror of Parthia', but 'friend of Parthia'; and IMPERATOR—not 'Roman commander', but 'commander against Rome'. This coin, Roman in appearance, was issued by a Roman who was Rome's enemy.

It was a general of Antony who defeated him. Antony, a Triumvir, shared the empire with Octavian (Lepidus, Pl. 2, no. 9, having been soon suppressed). Antony's legions, disposed about the eastern provinces, were celebrated one by one on a great series of coins (Pl. 14, no. 5). Though these pieces, like many others in later years (e.g. Pl. 15, no. 7), proudly show a Roman troop-carrying warship, the fleet on which Antony depended—in vain—was Cleopatra's. To the disapproval (no doubt) of his army commanders, who hated her, she herself appears with him on coins (Pl. 14, no. 6)—a prow before her portrait. She looks no beauty here (Pl. 10, no. 1 is rather more impressive); a far-fetched theory even suggests that the coin is enemy propaganda. She is described by the enigmatic title of 'Queen of Kings and of her Sons who are Kings'. These are eastern, Hellenistic titles; but her presence on the coin of a Triumvir suggests Roman ambitions too.

Antony's head here is accompanied by the Armenian royal tiara and the words ARMENIA DEVICTA—'Armenia Conquered.' The mighty Armenian mountains, with their ill-defined frontiers, were for centuries disputed between Rome and Parthia as they have been in modern times between Turkey and Russia. Repeated attempts by both the ancient empires to establish durable puppet regimes failed. One of those who tried was Antony, who ostensibly 'conquered' Armenia in 34 B.C. He celebrated a Triumph (at Alexandria! —that shocked Romans); the emphasis on conquest barely concealed a terrible retreat from the same country two years earlier, which had cost him more legionaries than he could afford. At least however, unlike Napoleon after Moscow, he was given a chance to improve appearances later, by his more successful or at any rate more impressive operations of 34 B.C., which this coin records.

The battle of Actium (31 B.C.), followed in the next year by the conquest of Egypt, gave Augustus sole control. But he did not put his generals to the supreme test of Armenia. Instead, through his stepson Tiberius (Pl. 32, no. 4), he undertook diplomatic negotiations with Parthia. They achieved a solution. But Augustus felt that Roman public, or senatorial, opinion must be presented with a victory: for he inscribes his coins ARMENIA CAPTA, Armenia 'captured', or sometimes RECEPTA, 'captured back' (Pl. 14, no. 7). Again the solution was sadly impermanent. After military conquest had persistently and expensively failed, it remained for the much-maligned Nero to create stability for decades by the simple expedient of making the Parthian nominee to the throne of Armenia, Tiridates, into the Roman nominee as well (p. 34).[1]

Though Augustus himself was no warrior, his relatives by marriage, and other generals, achieved solid military successes and added to the empire not only Egypt but vital regions in the Alps—Bavaria, Austria—and the Balkans. Other areas came into his empire by peaceful means: for example, a large tract of central Asia Minor was annexed after the death of its dependent monarch, and called the province of Galatia. But 'Victory', not peaceful annexation, was the talisman of Augustus (p. 22; Pls. 6, 7) and the quality which, despite his warnings against further expansion, all his successors wanted to inherit. Three centuries later, when barbarians were pressing the empire, the Christian Valens (soon to be defeated and killed by the Goths at Adrianople), still defines his role as 'triumphant over barbarous nations', TRIVMFATOR GENTIUM BARBARARUM (Pl. 17, no. 3). Emperors claimed to 'make the bounds of freedom wider yet', as Tennyson wrote when imperialism was still fashionable; though the Romans would especially have wished to provide, as well as freedom of a sort (Pl. 17, no. 2), greater security (Pl. 26, no. 5; cf. Pl. 8, no. 8).

Augustus' second stepson Nero Drusus not only joined his brother Tiberius in the conquest of Bavaria and Austria but made four attempts to advance the northern frontier beyond the Rhine. Fifty years after the death of Nero Drusus, his son Claudius commemorates his father's German trophies (DE GERMANIS) (Pl. 14, no. 8). The first stage was to have been the Elbe—not itself a good frontier, but on the way to the Vistula; optimists may have had even more distant goals in mind. Nero Drusus reached the Elbe once, but then he died. His son Germanicus achieved no more lasting success. So

[1] In the second century, anti-Parthian war-types return, e.g. Pl. 15, no. 5; cf. when Persians had superseded Parthians, Pl. 15, no. 7.

Roman Germany never again reached beyond the Lower Rhine [1]—no doubt to the regret of the amber-market in Rome (which it supplied) but also, it has been suggested by modern geopoliticians, with incalculable results for Europe. Roman hopes were finally eclipsed by the disaster in the Teutoburg Forest. The Roman Commander Publius Quinctilius Varus, whose force was ambushed and annihilated there by the German chieftain Arminius, had been portrayed earlier by a city in Africa during his governorship of that province (p. 62; Pl. 28, no. 2).

Provincial affairs took on a new aspect when Augustus' dynasty came to an end. For in the harrowing 'Year of the Four Emperors' (A.D. 69) it was rapidly and painfully learnt, by those who did not surmise it already, that provinces were not merely conquered territories but were countries with Roman governors who could supplant emperors chosen at home. On a Republican coin, Hispania, rent between Roman armies, had been shown as dishevelled and distressed (Pl. 14, no. 1). Now she is proudly standing (her name hardly visible on the left of this worn specimen) in front of Nero's successor Galba, on whom she is bestowing the Palladium, the revered statue of Minerva which symbolized Eternal Rome (Pl. 14, no. 10). For it was from Spain, and with Spain's legions, that Galba marched on Rome; and it was at the Spanish town of Clunia, explicitly mentioned on this coin, that he had waited until news came that he should leave for the capital. He is honouring here not so much the province as its Roman army, which had made him emperor.

The coins of another short-lived emperor of this period, Vitellius (Pl. 14, no. 11), clearly point the same unpalatable lesson, and remind the Senate that nominees of the provincial

[1] Beyond the Upper Rhine, the Black Forest, Neckar Basin and Swabian Alb were added before the end of the first century A.D.

armies could become emperors regardless of its wishes. It is true that Vitellius here stresses his 'Clemency'. But Clemency was to become an infrequent item in Roman coin propaganda, just because of associations with discreditable rulers such as Vitellius; and there is something disquieting about the inscription. The Clemency to which Vitellius lays claim is not called, as usual, 'the Clemency of the Augustus'—that is to say, of the reigning Augustus acting on the Augustan model —but is instead described as 'the Clemency of the Augustus who is Commander in Roman Germany' (CLEMENTIA IMP(*eratoris*) GERMAN(*ici*); on a parallel coin Victory is similarly represented. Beside the head of Vitellius the name 'Germanicus' is repeated. This designation had first been given after death to Nero Drusus because he had, allegedly, conquered Germany; now, however, it means the nominee of the legions stationed in that country.

But it was the legions in Judaea which equipped the successful contestant in the Civil Wars, Vespasian. A long and formidable Jewish revolt—issuing its own coinage (Pl. 15, no. 1)—had given him his chance of military power. When he reached Rome this success inspired one of the most famous geographical coin-types, 'Judaea Captured' (IVDAEA CAPTA) (Pl. 15, no. 2); the palm-tree symbolizes Judaea, as it once stood for India on our own coinage. There had been earlier 'types' of dejected countries and their symbols, but now the theme has culminated in a new artistic motif—the captive province.

Trajan, the greatest imperial aggressor, for a brief moment in A.D. 116 pushed the eastern frontier to Basra. But a more durable achievement—and for once a military operation which immediately paid its way—was his earlier conquest of Dacia (Rumania). Pl. 15, no. 3 provides a bird's-eye view, or symbolic sketch, of Trajan's great nineteen-pier bridge over the Danube into Dacia, near Drobetae (Turnul Severin). Inadequate as this representation is, it suggests the mechanics of Roman conquest and government: for implicit in the type are the great military roads behind the bridge and also far north of the Danube, as far as Porolissum (near Debrecen).

All this, and the emperor too, depended ultimately on the Roman army. Though coins say a good deal about imperial gifts to civilians (Pl. 20), they are tactfully silent concerning the great monetary bonuses which rulers lavished on the army. However, Hadrian issued a series of coins commemorating most of the major armies of the empire. One of them is the army of Spain, the country where his Italian ancestors had settled (Pl. 15, no. 4). This coin is inscribed EXERC(*itus*) HISPAN(*icus*), 'the army in Spain'. The emperor is seen on horseback addressing his legions. The design had occurred before, and was to be seen again (Pl. 16, no. 7). But this is the first time that the armies had been separately named; and such encouragement of their potential centrifugal tendencies has caused surprise. However, they are represented in purely Roman guise, without local differentiation.

Besides, Hadrian had a new conception of empire. I shall now go back to the beginning of the imperial regime and try to show how this new conception came about: how, alongside these types of conquest and military power, the emperors placed on their coinages a series of designs illustrating and developing a peaceful relationship with the provinces.

2. PEACE: ROME AND THE PROVINCES

Together with the gift of the Roman Peace itself, demonstrated to the world by innumerable coin-types, what endeared imperial rule to the provincials was its timely imperial benefaction. An early example is provided by Tiberius (Pl. 18, no. 1). He is represented as the civil and religious head of the Roman State—a seated figure, for out of official modesty he did not place his head on the largest brass coins of the capital. The inscription refers to 'the restoration of the communities of Asia' (CIVITATIBVS ASIAE RESTITVTIS). 'Asia' means the province of Asia, the heavily populated and urbanized western region of Asia Minor. Under Tiberius this country suffered earthquakes even more severe than the Erzincan disaster of 1940, the worst sufferer being Croesus' ancient capital Sardes (Sert) (A.D. 17). The emperor remitted taxes and provided huge sums for reconstruction.

But if benefactions were needed in the provinces, it was a hundred times more necessary that they should be lavishly granted at home. Thus Nero (Pl. 9, no. 2) displays a 'view' or sketch (our best surviving record) of Rome's port Ostia, in which gigantic improvements and enlargements had been undertaken by Claudius and were officially opened by Nero —who also, at about the time of this issue (c. A.D. 64), inaugurated a project (which came to nothing) to cut a 125-mile canal from Lake Avernus to Ostia. The harbour was called the Portus Augusti (POR. AVGVST.OST.). On the left is a crescent-shaped mole, with porticoes and hall at the end; on the right, a row of breakwaters or slips. The pillar at the top, with its statue, is the Pharos set at the entrance, like its famous prototype at Alexandria; and Neptune (or Father Tiber?) reclines below. This view of the Ostian harbour reminded all Romans (even those who could not read) that by its construction the emperors greatly facilitated the corn-supply from North Africa, and so helped to fill their stomachs. Nero was a good food-provider (p. 35), and so for a long time they loved him.

The benefactions recorded by later emperors sometimes refer to their removal of abuses. When, for example, after the suppression of the First Jewish Revolt (by Vespasian) (Pl.

15, nos. 1 and 2) Jews had been ordered to pay to Jupiter the silver piece previously paid to the temple at Jerusalem, lists of those liable had been drawn up with the distasteful aid of informers. The elderly ex-lawyer Nerva claims to have 'removed the false accusations employed for the Jewish tax' (FISCI IVDAICI CALVMNIA SVBLATA) (Pl. 18, no. 2)—though the tax itself remained. But here again it was advisable to remove abuses, and glorify the fact, in the nucleus of the empire, Italy. So Nerva 'remits to Italy the expenses of the imperial post' (VEHICVLATIONE ITALIAE REMISSA) (Pl. 18, no. 3); for Italian cities had suffered from the expensive journeys of his predecessor, Domitian. Now the mules are set free to graze, and the cart stands tilted and empty.

Nerva, though he was not strong enough to deal with a difficult political situation at Rome, helped Italy in other ways too. His great successor, Trajan, honoured by Senate and People as 'the best of rulers' (S.P.Q.R. OPTIMO PRINCIPI), celebrates Nerva's scheme for helping Italian orphans (the ALIM(enta) ITAL(iae)) (Pl. 18, no. 4). The scheme arranged for the orphans to be educated from the proceeds of land mortgages, for which the State advanced money at low rates of interest. This not only helped orphans; it also encouraged farming. So the figure protecting the child on the coin is Annona, goddess or personification of the corn-supply—and it is an ear of corn that she is holding. The water-supply at Rome was another matter that received Trajan's attention (Pl. 18, no. 5).

The previous section (p. 50) showed how the Roman government depicted provinces as conquered territories. But in the second century A.D. they began to be thought of in a more humane and co-operative spirit. For example Dacia (Rumania), though Trajan first shows her in the traditional dejection of defeat, later appears in a more hopeful and peaceful guise (Pl. 18, no. 6). As a 'province of the emperor' (DACIA AVGVST(*i*) PROVINCIA) she is shown in national dress (with pointed cap), accompanied by two children carrying grapes and corn—the crops of the future. Dacia is Rome's friend, and carries a Roman standard. Those who recall stories of Trajan's slaughters and deportations in Dacia have cause to doubt—yet it was at least a step forward that propagandists now felt a humane presentation to be necessary.

But it was the next reign that witnessed a sensational change. Hadrian loved Greek culture, and was the greatest imperial traveller that the world has ever known; most of his reign was spent in a series of royal tours. Himself a provincial from Spain, he thought of the empire as 'no mere system of dependencies, but a living organism, alive in all its parts, each sharing, each enjoying, the personal interest and care of emperors'. On an unparalleled series of coins he commemorated his own visits to no less than eighteen provinces or territories. Pl. 19, no. 1 celebrates his arrival in the province of Africa (Tunisia and Tripolitania): ADVENTVI AVG(*usti*) AFRICAE.[1] Another series shows Hadrian's 'restoration', by beneficent measures, of twelve countries: Pl. 19, no. 2 depicts him as Restorer of Gaul (RESTITVTOR GALLIAE).

On another great series he honoured, without fear, the provincial armies (p. 51; Pl. 15, no. 4). Yet another group of coins, issued at the same date, quite simply commemorates certain lands by name. BRITANNIA (Pl. 19, no. 3) shows that his programme was not expansive, like Trajan's, but defensive. He was not afraid to suggest that the provinces should themselves help in their own defence: so *Britannia* here displays her own national costume and shield. This is a new

[1] The theme of 'Adventus' remained an important one for centuries: Pls. 4, no. 6; 16, no. 6.

type, the *provincia vigil*, watching patiently over her northern hills—or is the object on which she rests her foot a symbolic representation of Hadrian's Wall?

His successor Antoninus Pius depicted a variant form of Britannia (Pl. 19, no. 4) which Charles II reproduced on his copper halfpennies. Frances Stuart, Duchess of Richmond, was requested to sit as a model; and there she and the design of Antoninus remain on British pennies today. But though Antoninus honoured provinces on the coinage, he thought that Hadrian had gone too far in this cosmopolitan and pro-Greek direction, and his own coinage soon settles down to a markedly Italian emphasis, with frequent evocations of antiquarian, Virgilian themes. Pl. 27, no. 3 shows Aeneas himself rescuing his father Anchises and his son Ascanius from burning Troy.

However, there was a strong reaction against this pro-Roman and pro-Italian policy later in the second century A.D., under Commodus (p. 70). At the end of a revolutionary reign, his non-Roman outlook caused him to reaffirm in far stronger form the cosmopolitanism of Hadrian, and even arrogantly to classify Rome, 'refounded' by him, as another 'colony of Commodus' (Pl. 19, no. 5). He is depicted in lion-skin as the reincarnation of Hercules [1]—who is seen, on the reverse, ploughing the foundation furrow, as it had been ploughed for many Roman settlements in the past (Pls. 6, no. 6; 22, no. 7).

After the ruinous civil wars that followed the death of Commodus (and had to be paid for), this centrifugal movement gained further force. For when the fierce victor Septimius Severus shows AFRICA on his coins in the national head-dress of an elephant's hide (Pl. 19, no. 6), this means no conquered province, not just another benefited territory, but

[1] Cf. Maximian later (Pl. 5, no. 5).

the country of the emperor's origin and special favour. Very few emperors were Italians nowadays, and under the almost totalitarian rule of Severus Italy was beginning to sink to the level of the provinces. A further step in this direction was taken by his wife's bizarre grand-nephew Elagabalus. Conducted from Syria to Rome at the age of fourteen (and renamed Marcus Aurelius Antoninus), Elagabalus imported with him the worship of which he had been hereditary priest at Emesa (Homs) (p. 43). His coins show the solemn procession of the Emesan sun-god, represented by a black stone; and the design is dedicated 'to the Holy Elagabalus, god of the Sun' (SANCT(*o*) DEO SOLI ELAGABAL(*o*), Pl. 21, no. 4). The proletariat enjoyed the exotic pageantry, but conservative national leaders could scarcely be pleased to see the Stone solemnly married to Minerva, who had so long been identified with Rome and its native traditions (Pl. 14, no. 9).

After the brief reign of Elagabalus there was a return to outward convention, but the progress of eastern beliefs was not arrested. And now Rome, hard-pressed by incessant foreign and civil wars which very nearly split the empire into fragments, plunged—to the misery of millions—into a bankruptcy recorded, and accelerated, by the rapidly debased coinage. The standard of living was beyond all rescue. But the empire itself was saved by a series of almost superhumanly able men produced, at this critical juncture, by the Illyrian and Danubian territories of the empire. The first and perhaps the least successful of them, Decius, duly records his homeland, the Pannonian provinces (PANNONIAE) (Pl. 19, no. 7). He sought to find a scapegoat for national disintegration by blaming the foreign sect of the Christians in the name of the old religion. Aurelian, from the same area, grafted on to the traditional cults Christianity's greatest rival, the widespread Oriental solar faith (Pl. 21, no. 6; cf. 5)—of which the deity of

Elagabalus was one local manifestation, and the officers' god Mithras a far more potent ally.

Further persecutions awaited the Christians. But then came the official volte-face under another Illyrian, Constantine the Great. The rise of Christianity to supremacy is duly recorded by the gradual appearance of its symbols on the coins (Pls. 21, nos. 7–10; 24, no. 10). Roman religion had succumbed to this cult from the eastern provinces: Galilee had conquered Rome.

CHAPTER IV

NEW EVIDENCE FOR THE PAST

1. UNKNOWN PEOPLE

HISTORIANS are not always willing to use the information that we numismatists claim to extract from our coins. They point out that our historical conclusions are frequently based on difficult and questionable arguments. Being more familiar with the literary evidence, they may well lack time and inclination to pursue this additional specialized study; so the information that coins supply is sometimes disregarded. Every numismatist can recall some recent historical work which, in his opinion, might have been more accurate or more informative if full use had been made of the coinage of that particular period and its political, economic, religious or artistic data. The historians may well object that, until numismatists learn more about their subject—and admittedly there is a vast amount still to be learned—it is safer not to accept evidence deduced from a coin unless it is confirmed by an ancient literary source. But this attitude ignores the positive, primary contributions made by coins, and is at the same time much too flattering to certain deficiencies and inadequacies of the ancient writers. They show a marked lack of interest in public finance. In particular, they rarely mention the coinage; and even when they do, they are often demonstrably inaccurate. So it is logical to go one step further and consider what the coins can teach us when no such literary comment is available.

To write the history of the chaotic third century A.D., the editors of the *Cambridge Ancient History* decided to call upon specialists on the coinage; and one of them, Harold Mattingly, described the coins as 'almost our only chance of penetrating the thick darkness that still envelops so much of the history of the third century'. Coins even reveal the names and features of men who are totally unknown to every surviving writer and, indeed, to any other source whatsoever. For example, no writer or inscription mentions Lucius Julius Aurelius Sulpicius Antoninus (Pl. 22, nos. 1 and 2). Other coins call him Uranius Antoninus; and provincial base silver and local bronze issues of Emesa (Homs), besides confirming the apparent self-description AVG(*ustus*) on Pl. 22, no. 1, add the Greek equivalent (*autokrator*) of the title *Imperator*. These titles indicate that he claimed the imperial throne—and dates on the local coins tell us when he did so: in A.D. 253–254.

There were many rebellions at this time, and historians mention a Uranius. But he had briefly revolted—in Mesopotamia—some twenty years earlier, so this cannot be he. The present Uranius evidently failed to secure a mention in our gravely inadequate historical record, the *Historia Augusta*; so he is known only from the coins. Conceivably he should be identified with a priest of Aphrodite said to have repulsed, before Emesa, the troops of Parthia's more formidable successors the Persian (Sassanid) monarchy. Possibly these coins show him trimming his sails: on the obverses there are no imperial titles, and though AVG. on the reverse of Pl. 22, no. 1 seems to refer to him, it is not certain whether the same word on Pl. 22, no. 2, and the reference to a first consulship, allude to himself or to the emperor Gallienus at Rome. At any rate, shadowy figure though Uranius is, it is the coins and not any literary records which have added him to history. The same is true of several other 'usurpers' of the later third century.[1]

---

[1] For instance, at least one and perhaps two usurpers called Domitianus are known only from coins.

Further completely unrecorded personages have been identified because of the Roman custom of depicting the wives of rulers on the coinage of their husbands (p. 38). This custom has bequeathed to history the otherwise unsuspected 'Augusta' Dryantilla (Pl. 22, no. 3). These are dreadfully in-artistic coins; both the portrait and the reverse type (Equity) seem like mere caricatures. But this was evidently an emer-gency issue. Parallel issues of the same style and the same find-sites show that her husband was a certain Regalianus (Pl. 22, no. 4), whom we know from literary sources to have usurped the purple for a few weeks in A.D. 260. The literary accounts locate his *coup d'état* on the lower Danube (in Moesia); but his coins and those of Dryantilla are found much farther west, in Austria—so that the numismatic evidence corrects the literary record, and shows that this is the area to which their brief rule has to be assigned.

Coins of finer style indicate that other women on the coin-age must have been the wives of Roman emperors ruling in the capital itself, though written history, as we have it, has again passed them by. One of these is Cornelia Supera Augusta. Her coin (Pl. 22, no. 5) displays the Roman type of Vesta—and a Roman style which decisively attributes it to the capital. The fabric and metal of her coins enable us to ascribe her to the decade immediately preceding Dryantilla's; and Cornelia has been identified, with a good deal of proba-bility, as the wife of an emperor who reigned at Rome for a short time in A.D. 253, Aemilianus (Pl. 16, no. 1). New also —except for an inscription—is a deified child Nigrinianus (Pl. 22, no. 6). It has been deduced that he was a son of Carinus (A.D. 283–284). One of the latter's numerous wives, too, has been identified as a certain Magnia Urbica (Pl. 13, no. 5), because her coins look like those of Carinus, and they are associated on medallions (non-monetary commemorative pieces, p. 65).

Once it is conceded that such coins have added (however little) to the sum of historical knowledge without any assistance from our literary authorities, then there is no longer any reason why every ancient and medieval coin should not be scanned by historians from the same point of view and pressed to disclose any secrets that it may hold. Often, it is true, the deductions to be drawn from them are still conjectural. Yet it is undeniable that Uranius and Cornelia Supera once lived, and it is only the coins that tell us so. With such concrete and indisputable results in mind, our approach to other numismatic evidence need not be too pessimistic.[1]

Nor is the third century the only epoch in which new personages can be discovered from the coinage. We also have portraits of completely unknown people at the beginning of the imperial epoch. Pl. 22, no. 7 is a small bronze piece known only from very few specimens. Its obverse inscription is M(*arcus*) RVTILVS PROCO(*n*)S(*ule*) COL(*onia*) IVL(*ia*). On the reverse is the name of Aulus Feridius, who is described as *duovir*, i.e. one of the leading officials of the community of citizen settlers which issued the coin: the status and title of the community, Colonia Julia, are mentioned. So this is one of that vast range of city-coinages of the Roman Empire (p. 73; Pls. 28, 30, 31). The coins come from Asia Minor, and I have argued elsewhere that the colony is Lystra (Hatunsaray, later visited by St Paul). On grounds of fabric, content and style it is agreed that this coin belongs to the revolutionary years in which the Roman Republic gave way to the imperial regime. But this unattractive and realistic portrait is not of Augustus or Antony or of any other famous leader: it must

[1] Coins give us the names of entirely unknown places as well as people, e.g. Came (Pl. 22, no. 8) and Tomara (Pl. 22, no. 9), both in Asia Minor and both probably to the south-east of Pergamum. Silerae, in Sicily, is known only from a coin of the fourth century B.C.

be Marcus Rutilus himself and, indeed, this is reasonable from the appearance of his name beside the head. The Civil Wars were a period when governors of provinces were led by ambition or circumstances to operate as semi-independent war-lords; and Rutilus, who has been identified with an officer mentioned in Julius Caesar's *Gallic War*, was very probably in this position. The reference to the colony as *Julia* shows that he supported Caesar against his enemies— or more probably supported Caesar's heirs against his assassins. At present that is all the information that these excessively rare coins can be made to yield—but no ancient author gives us even this much help.

Under Augustus we have further portraits of men not belonging to the imperial house (Pl. 28, no. 2). Here is the head of a man who is very well known indeed, but whose features were hitherto unknown to us. This is Publius Quinctilius Varus, later of ill-omened fame for the German ambush which cost him his life and army and Augustus his peace of mind (p. 49). But at this earlier stage he is proconsul of Africa (Tunis, etc.), and the name of the African city which thus issued coins in his honour is mentioned: it is Achulla. He was pro-consul in 8–7 B.C. or thereabouts. During a very short period at this time the governors both of Africa and of Asia, the two greatest 'senatorial' provinces left under ostensibly semi-independent proconsuls in the old Republican fashion, were simultaneously allowed by Augustus to have their own heads placed on local bronze coinages within their province. This simultaneous occurrence in African and Asia cannot be fortuitous. Besides, every one of the governors thus honoured was a friend, and relative by marriage, of the emperor— *amicus principis*. This designation was not yet official and hierarchic, as it was soon to become, but it already exalted men far above their fellows. Here, evidently, is a deliberately

concerted policy of honouring and pleasing the chief supporters of the regime and dynasty. The same phenomenon
briefly recurs, for similar reasons, under Tiberius, and also
elsewhere under Claudius (Pl. 31, no. 2). To this practice we owe
a number of sketches of men familiar to us from the pages of
Tacitus and Suetonius, but not from any portraits other than
those on the coins.

2. ART, POLITICS, RELIGION, ECONOMICS

The reverses of Roman and Graeco-Roman coinage provide
varied—though not always easily interpretable—contributions to the history of art. Much of this evidence is not
available from any other source. This was recognized two
hundred and fifty years ago by Addison (p. 17), who observed that 'the four most beautiful statues extant make their
appearance all of them on ancient medals'. A famous example
is the Zeus of Phidias at Olympia, on coins of the local mint
of Elis. These coins were issued under Hadrian, when art
took an antiquarian turn and the emperor himself posed as
Olympian Zeus. So the great statue is shown from various
angles on the coins. As representations of its artistic qualities,
such designs are of course wholly inadequate. But these
sketchy coin-types are of great value since they vitally supplement the descriptions of the masterpieces by writers such as
Pausanias.

Again, the numerous buildings which appear as the types
of Roman coins help greatly in determining the topography
of ancient Rome and the chronology of its main edifices. For
instance the antiquarian emperor Antoninus Pius shows us the
now vanished Temple of Augustus and Livia (Pl. 24, no. 3)
between the Palatine and the Capitol. By the word REST(*ituit*)
Antoninus explicitly states that he himself restored the

temple. He also gives us the dates of his restoration. The numbering of his 'tribune's power' (TR.P.XXII), reckoned annually from the year of his accession, indicates the year A.D. 158–159, and other similar pieces mention the immediately preceding year. Here then is the temple, with its restoration securely dated by the coinage.

The designers of such architectural types obeyed certain conventions—the exaggerated gap between the central columns is one of them—but these conventions vary within reasonably constant limits and they can be interpreted with benefit to archaeologists. For example, the façade on the present coin has been used to demonstrate that the temple cannot have been, as was thought, the building next door to the church of Santa Maria Antiqua. The temple has vanished (but across the Forum we can still possibly recognize the shrine of Romulus, the deified son of Maxentius, Pl. 24, no. 5).

Bluma Trell, in *The Temple of Artemis at Ephesus*, gives an instance of a vanished architectural feature that it has been possible to reconstruct from coins. A silver piece issued by Claudius in the province of Asia shows the temple of Artemis-Diana at Ephesus (DIAN. EPHE.) (Pl. 24, no. 2). The world-famous Ephesian temple, or rather its fourth-century B.C. restoration, has only survived in fragments, so any information that the coins may provide will be helpful. This coin shows a curious design in the pediment, including not only standing figures but also three rectangles. What are these? We cannot tell from the two surviving fragments of the pediment itself. But the answer is neatly provided by another coin, a Hadrianic local issue of a city in the same province, Magnesia on the Meander. It is poorly preserved, but examination reveals very similar rectangles; and we happen to know what these were. In the great second-century B.C. temple of Artemis at Magnesia, the pediment is known to have had

64

three doors or openings, which could be closed by wooden shutters; the cornices and frames of the openings have partially survived. The same openings must therefore have appeared on the temple at Ephesus. I must not discuss its purpose now, for my aim here is only to demonstrate that it is these two coins, of Claudius and Hadrian, which have enabled us to reconstruct an important architectural feature.

But greater contributions to the history of art are made by that astonishing range of portraiture which has always been considered the chief glory of Roman coinage. To take one out of very many examples, a gold coin of the third-century Gallic usurper Postumus, issued probably at Colonia Agrippina (Cologne), shows a remarkable three-quarter-face portrait (Pl. 24, no. 6) inspired, it may well be, by a painting rather than by a sculptural model. This fine head—noteworthy at a time of political and economic misfortunes—is valuable material for those art-historians who discuss the development and origins of these frontal and semi-frontal portraits. Here we have an early anticipation of the full Byzantine 'frontality' (Pl. 26, nos. 9 and 10), just as the Arches of Severus at Rome and Lepcis Magna earlier in the same century have pointed the way to other Byzantine motifs. Quite exceptionally, a fully frontal bust had occurred on a Roman bronze medallion even in the previous century, under Commodus, but unfortunately the only specimen known to me, that in the British Museum, is very worn.[1] Roman commemorative medallions (p. 60) have particular value to the art-historian since their conventions are less strict than those of the coinage, so that more variety is possible in their designs (Pls. 3, no. 5; 5, nos. 4, 5, and 7; 15, no. 7; 16, nos. 7 and 8; 17, nos. 1 and 3; 19, no. 8; 20, no. 3; 27, no. 4).

---

[1] Small frontal heads occur under Severus—and on a rare, ill-preserved coin of Caligula at Apamea in Bithynia (Pl. 28, no. 3). Those portrayed are in both cases women; cf. later, Pl. 13, no. 9.

For our knowledge of the politics, as well as the art, of this separatist empire which Postumus founded in Gaul and the western provinces, the numismatic evidence is exceptionally important. The coins provide, among much else, the actual limits of date for this empire (A.D. 258–259 to 274), and they also provide the correct order of the five rulers who controlled it. Two of these 'emperors', Victorinus and Tetricus, are shown on Pl. 16, nos. 2 and 3.

Soon after the empire of Postumus ended, another short-lived independent regime began in Britain, under Carausius (A.D. 288–293) (Pl. 23, nos. 1–4) and Allectus (A.D. 293–296) (Pl. 23, no. 5).[1] Postumus had visited Britain, and Carausius modelled himself on him—as a curiously medieval-looking imitation of his three-quarter-face portrait (Pl. 24, no. 7) suggests. Carausius coined at London (M.L.=Moneta Londinensis) and perhaps Bitterne (C.=Clausentum?). Some of his issues enable us to reconstruct a lost chapter of history by telling us of the peace he succeeded in extorting from Rome. We find the inscription PAX AVGGG.—'the Peace of the Emperors'—with the final letter twice repeated, indicating that three emperors are mentioned. The other two are the central rulers Diocletian and Maximian, and all three appear together on some of Carausius' coins (Pl. 23, no. 1). We know from the literary record that, when he abandoned his imperial command and turned pirate, he defeated Maximian at sea; and these coins show that he extorted at least outward recognition from him and Diocletian. He even describes them as his 'brothers'—the heads are labelled CARAVSIVS ET FRATRES SVI—and he also issued coins in the names of each of them

[1] Britain again became the base of usurpations when governors, Magnus Maximus (A.D. 383–388) (Pl. 23, no. 6) and Constantine III (A.D. 407–411), invaded the Continent and sought, successfully in the former case, to reach Rome.

separately (Pl. 23, no. 3). But though the historian Aurelius Victor concedes that Carausius was 'allowed to rule', the so-called brothers did not reciprocate on the coinage of their own territories. We know that for a time Carausius controlled Northern France; and coin-finds enable us to draw a line across Gaul indicating the limits beyond which his coins did not circulate, and so beyond which, apparently, his flimsy agreement with the central emperors ceased to be valid.

The coins of Carausius also provide other inscriptions which add to our total store of information—or of problems. One of these inscriptions is very familiar from earlier reigns: it is SAECVLARES AVG(*usti*) (Pl. 23, no. 2). According to abundant precedent this should refer to a celebration of the great Secular Games, which were staged in Rome (at elaborately determined dates) to purify the taints of the past and install a new Golden Age—that dominant theme of later imperial publicity (Pl. 25). But Carausius did not rule at Rome, we know of no Secular celebration by him, and the latest such celebration of which we have any record took place more than a generation before his reign. However, he was very Roman in his claims (Pl. 23, no. 4); did he perhaps arrange a celebration of the Games in his capital and mint-city London? We do not know; as, indeed, we know next to nothing of what happened at these outlying courts of usurpers. But the coins of Carausius raise the question; and so does a similar design under the earlier usurper Uranius Antoninus (Pl. 22, no. 2).

The last documented celebration of the Secular Games was that of Philip in A.D. 248, for the millenary of Rome (Pl. 25, no. 5), calculated from 753 B.C. We also know that Claudius had celebrated these Games 200 or, rather, 201 years earlier. In the intervening century, under Antoninus Pius in A.D. 148, there was no official Secular celebration; but we learn that this 900th anniversary was informally celebrated—and emphatically celebrated, as one would expect under so traditionalist an emperor. The Berlin coin collection possessed a brass medallion of the year, which surely refers to the celebration. It shows a processional chariot, displaying a statue inscribed R O M(*a*) and a relief of Romulus and Remus and the wolf. This medallion is dated to A.D. 148, the very year of the centenary: students of the piece agree that so entirely exceptional a design must relate to the anniversary occasion.[1]

I have stressed this point because it helps to enlarge our methods of research. It is sometimes complained that the historical allusions which we numismatists see in coins and medallions are often so indirect, so inexplicit, that they are dubious (p. 58). But here is an example, and I think there are many more, of an historical allusion being pretty certain in spite of its indirectness. Contemporaries, if they belonged to circles well versed in such matters, did not require references as direct as those needed by ourselves, at our distance of so many centuries; it was contrary to the traditional form of Roman coins and medallions to make everything explicit.

Thus we seem to have allusions to the 900th anniversary of Rome in A.D. 148 as well as to its 1000th in A.D. 248. Harold Mattingly has suggested that a major monetary reform may also have accompanied the next centenary after that, in A.D. 348. On the coinage of Constans (Pl. 25, no. 7) there is an inscription, familiar in substance but new in formulation, 'The Recovery of Happy Times'—F E L (*icium*) T E M P (*orum*) R E P A R A T I O—a highly appropriate slogan for such an anniversary. Moreover, these coins included a new bronze denomination: such changes were often timed to coincide with jubilees. If the attribution to the centenary is accepted, it indicates that Romans cele-

[1] Coins of Antoninus alluding to celebrations at about this time (Pl. 25, no. 1) may well refer to the same occasion.

brated this 1100th anniversary; such a celebration was certainly to be expected, but is not otherwise known.

But this inscription 'The Recovery of Happy Times' constrains us to be a little cynical about certain coin-types. Not only do they record events; they also record programmes. They provide pious hopes, wishful thinking, and downright lies—a common feature of propaganda at many epochs. In the unhappy Year of the Four Emperors, Otho, whose reign is a byword for its unpeaceful brevity, proudly displays the inscription 'Peace throughout the World'—PAX ORBIS TERRARVM (Pl. 26, no. 1). There was no Peace; the coin tells us of no historical fact. Instead, it brings to our attention a singularly unrealizable element in the imperial programme and publicity. Similarly, in the civil wars of the same year and of A.D. 193, and in the more lasting disorders of the third century, we have repeated reference to the high morale of the disaffected army (Pl. 26, nos. 2 and 4), the complete security of the utterly insecure regime (Pl. 26, no. 5) and the mutual affection of co-emperors who hated each other (Pl. 26, no. 6). The primary function of the coins is to record the messages which the emperor and his advisers desired to commend to the populations of the empire—whether facts, or aspirations, or lies.

As I suggested in connection with Nero (p. 27), this becomes a function of particular value when our literary tradition is hostile to an emperor. The writers dislike Domitian; but his fine coinage (Pl. 4, no. 2) increases our understanding of his policy and publicity. For instance, Pl. 27, no. 2 prominently displays the title *Germanicus*, and there is also a distinctive device of German shields and arms. This coin shows that, as conqueror of Germany—as *Germanicus*—he presented himself as the direct heir of the first *Germanicus*, namely Augustus' stepson Nero Drusus (p. 48): it was to the latter that the name was first awarded (posthumously) after his pioneer invasions of Germany had won him great popularity (despite their insubstantial results). Moreover, this highly distinctive design had appeared on only one Roman coin before, and that was a posthumous issue for Nero Drusus himself (Pl. 27, no. 1). That coin is exactly copied by Domitian. The resemblance cannot be fortuitous. Nor, presumably, did Domitian's contemporaries fail to notice that he assumed the title *Germanicus* in the 100th year after Drusus' first great victories. These coins suggest, then, that Domitian (or his advisers) found it possible to present him in the central tradition of imperial Roman conquerors of Germany. Our literary sources do not agree; but perhaps there is some truth on both sides.

Another emperor who secured a 'bad press' from the writers is Commodus (Pl. 27, no. 5). Historical tradition describes continuous personal misconduct combined with exotic religious aberrations. The coins, on the other hand, display a coherent religious policy based on Roman tradition yet not excluding oblique references to the ever-increasing influence of Oriental religions: by implication their central themes are deliberately incorporated into the Roman tradition, which thus comes to be expressed in almost monotheistic terms. So Jupiter, whose grandeur had already been stressed in the previous reign (Pl. 27, no. 4), is given by Commodus an unprecedentedly emphatic title of supremacy: EXSVPER. (*exsuperatorius* or *exsuperantissimus*). This Jupiter, it has been said, transcends the idea of a national god; he has become the centre of a universal system of divinities that restored to a divided world an elemental unity. Though the coins must not be regarded as cancelling or superseding the literary record, they show how the climate of opinion was preparing for the further spread of monotheistic faiths, culmnating in Christianity. Much light still remains to be thrown on the religious representations on coins, and if this can be done we may be able to add appreciably to our knowledge of what the Romans believed and felt.

I have suggested here a very few of the ways in which coins can throw light on the history of ancient art, politics and religion.[1] There is much, too, that might be said concerning their value to economic historians. Here I shall restrict myself to a single, concrete aspect—the information that they give us about the organization of the mint and the currency. Early Byzantine coins—to borrow an example from Philip Grierson—reveal facts about mint-administration which no writer has told us. We have no written record of mint-organization in early Byzantine times, but from the coins we learn that early in the sixth century the mint of Constantinople was organized in ten departments (*officinae*) for the issue of gold. Thus gold pieces of Justin I (Pl. 26, no. 9) bear the signature of the tenth of those departments: after the main reverse inscription VICTORIA AVGGG.[2] appears the Greek numeral I(*iota*) = 10. In precisely similar fashion we can deduce that the bronze issues of Constantinople were issued by five departments. For on large bronze coins of Justinian I (Pl. 26, no. 10) the numerals run from A, one, to E, five. This specimen of Justinian also reminds us that coins occasionally reveal the organization of the currency itself, its division into denominations. For the large M is the Greek numeral for forty indicating that this bronze piece (the *follis*) contained forty of a small unit (the *noummion* or *nummus*).

At an earlier date such information is equally significant and definite. Pl. 26, no. 8 shows a silver coin of Diocletian,

[1] For the invasion of Rome by foreign religions, see also p. 56.

[2] I.e. *Augustorum*, 'of the imperial pair'. Earlier the presence of three Gs had signified three *Augusti*, but during the fifth century that significance had disappeared.

issued at Aquileia in North Italy at the time of his currency-reform shortly before A.D. 300.[1] Among the grave economic probems of this reform a fixed point is the numeral XCVI on the silver issues, which Diocletian had just revived after coinage in this metal had long been in abeyance[2]. The numeral indicates that these unitary pieces, even though struck under weight, were intended to be current at the rate of ninety-six to the Roman pound (as had the older imperial *denarii*, before the inflations of the third century). Similarly, Diocletian's gold coins show Greek numerals, first seventy and then sixty, indicating the fractions of the pound which they too represented. Our literary sources leave so many aspects of this monetary reform obscure that such information from the coinage itself is of great value.

[1] Diocletian's capital was at Nicomedia, Pl. 27, no. 7.
[2] Carausius (p. 67) had briefly revived it in Britain.

CHAPTER V

APPROACH TO WORLD COINAGE

I. A GREAT NETWORK OF MINTS

THE Romans were faced with a mighty currency problem. Not even Alexander the Great (Pl. 1, no. 8) had been offered the task—and the political and economic advantage—of supplying coinage to so large an area of the civilized world. For centuries the Roman emperors provided their vast and heterogeneous empire with sufficient coinage for its needs; and they rarely made the mistake of sacrificing efficiency to uniformity. So there was a bewildering multitude of different monetary arrangements in different regions, and, in any one area, many different sorts of coin could coexist.

In the first place, great quantities of base-metal token-pieces were issued by local (not imperial) authorities at hundreds of different centres. Cities all round the Mediterranean coasts had for a very long time issued their own coins (Pl. 1). Under Augustus the mints issuing city-coinages of silver had diminished to a mere handful, but not less than 300 towns in the Roman Empire struck their own bronze coinage. Later this number considerably increased, and with various fluctuations in number and bulk these city-issues continued during the first three centuries of the imperial regime.

No historian can effectively study any Roman emperor's reign unless he has a good knowledge of the local coinages issued in all parts of the empire during that reign. But a second, and contradictory, consideration is this: he can, at present, only with the utmost difficulty obtain that knowledge. Attempts to compile *empire-wide* descriptions of local coinages for any given period have so far been extremely rare. There are studies of a single region,[1] or a single town, but even these are far from complete. Many coins are still unpublished. Just by sitting patiently in the bazaar at Adana for the duration of several cups of coffee one is very often able to see coin after coin which has never yet been described.

Or for Adana read Tunis, or Salonica, or Damascus. For there were flourishing city-coinages under the empire not only in Asia Minor, but in North Africa and Spain—for a time—and for a very long time in the Balkans and Syria. The coinages of Syrian towns (Pl. 30, no. 7) were particularly varied and long-lived. They are also ill-preserved, wretchedly inartistic, often rare nowadays, and extremely hard to interpret. Many problems are raised by the multiplicity of the chronological systems which they employ. Yet they are capable, precisely for that reason (among others), of providing historical information.

The most remarkable region of the empire for local bronze coinages is Asia Minor. It contained, in certain areas, more towns than are to be seen now. Under Augustus about ninety-seven of them issued their own coinage; and in the second and third centuries the total increased to 312 or more (though not all the mints were active simultaneously). The designs and inscriptions of these coins constitute a vast and largely unexplored mine of historical facts.

The most abundant city-coinage comes from the western quarter of the peninsula, the once enormously prosperous province of Asia itself (Pl. 31)[2]. By the time of Augustus the area prolific in coinage had come to include the hinterland of Phrygia, developed and urbanized quite recently, in Hellen-

[1] For instance, the superb series of British Museum Catalogues of Greek coins.   [2] Cibyra (Pl. 31, no. 2) was not always in the province.

istic times. Passing through Phrygia today one can see by the roadside, or on the horizon, the unexcavated mounds that still conceal the wealthy cities ruled by pro-Roman oligarchies. Fashions may turn again from earlier sites, and we may see excavators unearthing the art collections of rich Phrygian friends of Roman emperors.

But there were also many city-mints in other parts of the Asian province, nearer the coasts—in towns of every degree of privilege. The number and output of these mints gradually increased. Many coinages show heads of Augustus, but these are often posthumous. In his reign seventy-three mints of the province (out of the ninety-seven for the whole peninsula) seem to have issued bronze coins; but some of these were issued in small quantities for special occasions, such as the festivals which many towns held in the emperor's honour every four years. The currency of the Asian cities began to attain an impressive bulk under Claudius. In the second century it increased further; during the third century the output was enormous—and the number of mints in the province had risen to 168, even more than half the total for Asia Minor (Pl. 31, nos. 4–7).

All over the East the inscriptions of city coinages were in Greek, except at the organized 'colonies' of Roman citizen settlers. But these citizen communities were scarce in the East: they were far more numerous in the West. Under the first emperors many such western towns coined bronze—one in Gaul, Nemausus (Nîmes) (Pl. 28, no. 1), on a gigantic scale which must owe much to imperial initiative. In Spain, too, some thirty Roman communities (as well as native towns, Pl. 30, no. 1) issued coins under Augustus and his successors, sometimes only on special occasions and anniversaries, but often in substantial quantities. Yet not one of these Spanish coinages outlasted the first three imperial reigns. The local mints seem to have been restricted by Caligula (c. A.D. 39). This was partly for economic reasons, in order to centralize this important function, but partly—and perhaps in the first instance—because the flattery of the imperial family in which these citizen communities extravagantly indulged (more extravagantly than the imperial mints)[1] had become unacceptable to Caligula: for after at first honouring all his relatives, alive and dead (e.g. Augustus, Pl. 30, no. 2), he had subsequently taken a dislike to them.

In the East, where no such ban was imposed on the few and scattered citizen communities, we have an example of such flattery at Apamea in Bithynia. This town honours Caligula's three sisters (Pl. 28, no. 3); coinages at Rome had done the same, but Apamea goes further by calling his favourite, Drusilla, a goddess (DIVA). She had been deified after her death at Rome, but there had never been an imperial goddess before, and the conservative Roman coinage is silent concerning the event. However, the citizens overseas at Apamea had no such qualms.

Another citizen community in the East which still coined under Caligula is Patrae (Patras) in Greece, COL.A.A.P. = *Colonia Augusta Aroe Patrensium* (Pl. 28, no. 4). The date can be determined because the chariot on the reverse is imitated from Roman mintages in honour of Germanicus; and those have, on independent grounds, been rightly ascribed to the reign of his son Caligula. This borrowing of Roman models by local coinage is characteristic of citizen colonies, where the inhabitants often ignore local cults or interests and derive their coin-types from far-off Rome (cf. Vesta at Apamea, Pl. 28, no. 3).

---

[1] The portrayal of *local* notables is very rare: e.g. Diogenes the Cynic at Sinope, Pl. 28, no. 5. Cf. Pythes, member of a local ruling family at a non-Roman community, Laodicea, Pl. 31, no. 1.

This specimen from Patrae is exceptionally rare. It is also, for a local and eastern issue, an exceptionally large piece. I suspect that it was commemorative, not unlike our Crown pieces. Indeed, it may be particularly comparable to our coronation-Crowns. For many ancient pieces celebrated imperial accessions; and the accession of Caligula conveniently occurred in the very year in which Patrae celebrated its half-centenary as a colony. But most significant of all is the obverse inscription, INDVLGENTIAE AVGVSTI MONETA IMPETRATA—a grateful dedication 'to the Indulgence of the new emperor because the right to issue coinage had been requested by Patrae and granted'. For a town to have its own coins was clearly a privilege—partly for honorific reasons, but also because the cities were allowed to attach enhanced token-values to these bronze currencies, so that those privileged to issue them made a profit.

Sometimes the issuers were not the single cities of a province, but their combined representatives sitting at the Provincial Assembly (*Commune*), sanctioned by the emperors and devoted to the maintenance of their worship. Under Hadrian, the Bithynians display the temple they have erected for this purpose (Pl. 28, no. 7). Cyprus prefers to show its ancient temple of Aphrodite at Paphos (Pl. 28, no. 8).

But when bronze coins have been issued in the name of a province, the responsible authority is often not the *Commune* but the governor. That is to say, the coins are issued by the representative of the Roman State. But to distinguish them from the less localized main imperial coinage they may conveniently be described as 'provincial'. Provincial issues of the early emperors often bear little evidence of their character and origin; and I have spent much time in museums trying to disinter them from coin-trays marked 'uncertain', or, what is even more confusing, from rows of *city*-coinages ('local') from which (in view of their different administrative origins) they ought to be kept apart.

The inscriptions on provincial bronze are either in Greek or in Latin, according to the language predominant in the area. One short-lived Latin group was issued by the governors of Dacia (Rumania) (Pl. 29, no. 5). This is dated according to a provincial era starting not with the annexation of the province under Trajan but long afterwards under Philip the Arabian (A.D. 246). The type is Dacia personified, holding the standards of the garrison's two legions: their emblems, the eagle and lion, are also to be seen. But this provincial mint ceased its activity after only eleven years, owing to one of the military shocks which preceded the final evacuation of the province. Usually we have little or no idea why sporadic provincial issues occur, but in this case the motive seems to have been encouragement of a gravely ravaged province, and response to an urgent need; for the collapse of communications had begun to prevent the great imperial token-issues from reaching the more distant parts of the empire.

By the time of Philip these great imperial series had decayed in weight and metal, but in their beginnings under Augustus they had been very impressive. Roman popular opinion under the Republic had never fully grasped or accepted the token principle; and when the Republican government, in financial straits and short of the tin that was needed for bronze coinage, had repeatedly reduced the size and weight of its unattractive bronze issues, Romans had evidently objected so strongly that for half a century before Augustus their mint had ceased to issue them at all. This must have been very inconvenient; but then Augustus had the excellent idea of abandoning the muddy colour of the discredited bronze and issuing his token-coinage in bright golden-yellow brass (*orichalcum*)—Julius Caesar had first made the experiment (Pl. 26, no. 7)—and also in deep red, un-alloyed copper. Augustus was a master of psychology, and his coinage was a success; its light weight may have earned him considerable profits.

In the West his huge coinage in brass and (especially) copper at Lugdunum (Lyon) appealed to provincial loyalty by displaying the altar of Rome and Augustus, which provided the regional centre for emperor-worship (Pl. 29, no. 2). But this series scarcely outlived him, and it was the series inaugurated by him at Rome itself (Pl. 7, no. 1) which gained acceptance. Indeed, it continued to be acceptable for many years, until hard-pressed emperors of the third century debased the metals, spoilt the fine appearance of the coins, and so weakened still further the public confidence which was already undermined by the debasement of the silver value-money and the consequent flooding of the market by inferior metal.

Some of the main official token-coinages of brass and copper were struck in millions, others were issued in small quantities and for special purposes. Among the former, still surviving in great numbers throughout western Europe, are copper pieces, representing Victory, issued by Nero at Rome (Pl. 8, no. 5) and at another active mint, usually attributed to Lugdunum. The political messages on such coins have a special interest, since these were the issues and these the designs selected for mass-circulation. On the other hand, some coins in the imperial series are so rare that they are almost comparable with the non-monetary medallions (pp. 60, 65).

The brass and copper coinage used to be known as 'senatorial', because of the prominent allusion to a senatorial decree (s.c.=*senatus consulto*) which habitually appeared on it. Yet the ultimate control of the coinage did not belong to the Senate any more than it belonged to the very junior Board of Three who presided at the mint. The coinage was controlled not by them but by the emperor. He preferred, however, to operate through strictly traditional forms (p. 24). That is why s.c., still referring to the Roman Senate, can appear also on other large token coinages which were mostly issued in the important province of Syria, though it was administered direct by the emperor as an 'imperial' province —that is to say, it was not a 'senatorial' province administered by proconsuls (p. 62). Partly for purposes of pseudo-Republican display, and partly for the sake of administrative efficiency, these decrees of the Senate were allowed to apply not only to 'senatorial' but also to 'imperial' provinces. So the main area of mintage and circulation of these eastern token-pieces with s.c. remained, for well over two centuries, 'imperial' Syria.

Yet these coins cannot possibly be dismissed, as most catalogues dismiss them, as mere local issues. They are not local in either sense—they are neither the products of a mere city-mint, nor are they of narrowly limited circulation. The bulk of output was often enormous: for instance, at the remote city of Dura Europos in Mesopotamia the finds include 163 pieces of Claudius alone, and as many as 434 (including halved pieces) of the single short reign of Elagabalus (Pl. 29, no. 4). This bulk suggests an imperial plan; and the letters s.c. confirm the supposition. Yet the coins ignore, from the very beginning, the elaborate balance of brass and copper established in the West. Here, in Syria and the East, Italy's historical objections to bronze were evidently lacking; so the eastern coins are of bronze. This, then, is a great imperial issue which is adapted with complete elasticity to the requirements of the eastern provinces.[1]

---

[1] But we are almost entirely in the dark about the metrological systems employed for eastern bronze. The coinage of Rhodes provides an occasional clue: Pl. 30, no. 3 is labelled *didrachmon* (2-drachm piece).

Coinage in the precious metals presents a simpler empire-wide picture, since the circulation of *aurei* and silver *denarii* was almost unlimited. It is true that certain of them do not appear in very widely distributed finds. For example, the issues of Augustus' general Publius Carisius at Emerita for the Spanish campaigns (25–22 B.C.) (Pl. 29, no. 1) circulates rather sluggishly elsewhere in the empire. But that is an exception, indeed a survival from the revolutionary days when generals signed their own coinage. In only one country were there arrangements of an imperative and exclusive character: *denarii* were not allowed into Egypt. A special preserve of the emperor—immensely important owing to its corn-surplus—Egypt was not allowed to admit this basic part of the official currency. Instead of silver it had, from Tiberius onwards, base silver or billon (Pl. 10, nos. 4 and 5),[1] unfavourably rated in relation to the *denarius*.

The emperor based this and other eastern silver issues not on the Roman system but on various standards inherited from the Hellenistic States which had preceded the Roman empire. Cyprus, Crete (Pl. 30, no. 2), Syria, Phoenicia, and various parts of Asia Minor (Pls. 6, no. 8; 29, no. 3) all provided mints for this purpose. Their issues are distinct and differently based; and all have to be taken into account if we are to appreciate the full scope, complexity and elasticity of the imperial currency.

2. BEYOND THE FRONTIERS

The imperial currency circulated on a vast scale beyond the imperial frontiers; it was, indeed, almost a world coinage. Perhaps no coins circulated so widely and in such large

[1] In the third century, the silver element disappeared completely (Pl. 29, no. 6), even before the same thing happened at Rome (p. 79).

quantities as the gold and silver of Augustus bearing the figures of his grandsons Gaius and Lucius (Pl. 32, no. 1). For example, these pieces are frequently found in what is now Soviet Armenia—which was, in ancient times, the eastern nucleus of the Armenian kingdom. The presence of imperial coinage here is not surprising since Rome continually sought to outbid Parthia's claims to the territory. However, the same coins are also discovered in great abundance in the remoter region to the north of the present Soviet Armenia—namely eastern Georgia. But this area too was part of the Augustan *cordon sanitaire*. It contained the small semi-dependent kingdom of Iberia. This was not one of the grand client-kingdoms like the Crimean Bosphorus to the north-west (Pl. 32, no. 9); Iberia was patriarchal and somewhat primitive. But it was the most advanced territory in the Caucasus, and it was significantly situated.

Here the motive for Rome's interest could again be regarded as political: to win the favour of another State against the Parthians, whose supporters Augustus' grandson Gaius was resisting at the time of his death (A.D. 4). But the motive may also have been partly economic. For Roman businessmen were at this time exceedingly eager, to satisfy the vast appetites of the rich, to secure silk; and of silk the Chinese had a monopoly. In Yarkand (Sinkiang) and Tashkurghan (northern Afghanistan) middlemen exchanged Chinese silk for Roman precious stones. But the main route westwards was by land over Parthian territory, and Parthia hated this trade between Rome and China. It was possible to travel north of Parthia, across the Caspian; but even when the Caspian had been crossed, the main route, through the Araxes valley (Aras), was again dangerously liable to intervention from Parthia. Farther north, however, there was an alternative route, out of Parthian reach. After crossing the Caspian one could turn in a more northerly direction, traversing the Caucasus by river (the Kura), road and again river to Phasis on the Black Sea—only one day's sail from Trapezus (Trebizond). This route through the Caucasus passed straight through Iberia; and that may have been one of the reasons why the Romans poured *denarii* into that little country—to make and keep the road clear for the transport of the silk which the governing class wanted.

The gold and silver coins with these designs form a coinage of vast dimensions. It is not easy to say where Augustus had minted the pieces which streamed into eastern Armenia and Iberia. One large mint for the series was Lugdunum (Lyon) in Gaul, but there may have been mints nearer at hand; there were many soldiers in Syria who had to be paid. Even in the West, Lugdunum may not have been the only mint. Dies of these coins have been found at Calagurris (Calahorra) in northern Spain; they seem to me genuine official products. Find-sites for dies have hitherto been mostly western; but this may be fortuitous—and there is a certain tendency among western scholars, who have not access to less known Levantine and Anatolian coin-finds, to ignore the possibility of eastern mints. However, the location of the mints of these great gold and silver issues is a problem for the future. They were augmented by local and unofficial efforts. With or without imperial approval they were widely imitated, in more or less barbaric styles, within the empire and beyond its frontiers (Pl. 32, no. 2; cf. no. 3).

Even farther afield than the Caucasus, in southern India, similar Augustan silver coins are again found in large quantities. Here there are even more numerous finds of a *denarius* of Tiberius (Pl. 32, no. 4). This is the so-called 'Tribute Penny' of the Bible. It is identified with the 'penny' that was brought to Jesus (Matt. xxii. 15–22, Mark xii. 13–17, Luke xx. 20–6).

No other *denarius* of Tiberius circulated nearly so extensively. In particular, these pieces are found in astonishing numbers, amounting to many hundreds, in one not very large area between Mysore and Travancore, namely Coimbatore. Why? Partly, perhaps, because beryls were mined there, and merchants knew that Roman women were extremely eager to obtain beryls for their ear-rings. They valued beryls and opals only less than diamonds (which they could rarely obtain) and emeralds, especially for ear-drops.

But the most likely reason for the preponderance of Roman coins in this area of southern India is the cultivation of pepper. Pepper was a greatly prized item in the metropolitan diet. When Alaric sacked Rome nearly four centuries later, he demanded 3000 lb. of it; and it was because the Dutch raised the price of pepper that the East India Company was founded in 1599. Now this was the richest spice-producing region of India: great pepper estates spread over its lower altitudes. The encyclopaedic scientist Pliny the Elder could not think why people liked pepper, but he realized that it played a principal part in the annual drain of Roman bullion to India. In order to pay for their pepper, westerners offered wine, or even no cargo at all—except these coins as a means of exchange, or even as bullion. Using the south-west monsoon (understood from about the time of Augustus), many such ships came straight from Arabia to the main port of south-western India, Muziris (Cranganore), to be loaded with pepper from the interior.

At least three, perhaps four, embassies from India came to Augustus; and they included delegations from the south. They brought expensive presents. One of their principal aims was to facilitate the journeys of foreign traders in their country. Here there was evidently a difficulty in Coimbatore. The abandonment of so many hoards indicates that conditions must have been troubled. There is a tradition that the frontiers of three warring Tamil kingdoms met in this area. Moreover, the principal road from west to east passed through the Coimbatore 'gap', where the coins have been found. This road was tempting to bandits, for western business-men interested in the pepper and beryl trades went this way. Some of them no doubt abandoned these *denarii*, in the unfulfilled hope of later recovery. Other traders, even more adventurous, may have travelled along this road towards the Bay of Bengal, in the hope of buying muslin; for the land-route, however dangerous, was preferable to the circumnavigation of Cape Comorin.[1] In the whole of this area the coinage of Tiberius and Augustus predominates. The scarcity of later pieces is due to Roman restrictions on the drain of bullion and perhaps especially to one of the results of that drain, a debasement of the silver coinage by Nero (*c.* A.D. 64), which is likely to have caused a *crise de confiance* in India.

Convoys of ships bound for India, with archers to protect them, sailed straight across the Indian Ocean—thus avoiding coastal pirates. They started from Aden (Arabia Eudaemon), which had a second important function: it served the South Arabian State of Saba (Sheba), which provided one of what Sir Mortimer Wheeler calls 'the five mainsprings of Roman long-range trade',[2] namely incense. Saba's communications with the Roman empire, via Petra, lay (until Egypt provided an alternative route) through an important protectorate in the north-west of the Arabian peninsula, the kingdom of the

[1] Sir Mortimer Wheeler has excavated a remarkable commercial centre at the eastern extremity of this land-route (Arikamedu in Pondicherry).

[2] He identifies the others as amber (from free Germany), ivory (from Africa), silk and pepper.

Nabataeans; and Nabataean troops guarded the road. This State extended as far as Damascus to the north, and included nearly all Sinai, and the Hejaz for about one-third of the way down its coast. The Nabataeans, though dependent on Rome, had their own coinage (Pl. 32, no. 6)—like their unfriendly northern neighbour Herod the Great in Israel and Jordan (Pl. 32, no. 5), and other client-kingdoms (Pl. 32, nos. 7–9). The Nabataeans, like Herod, were independent enough to dispense with mention of Augustus on their coins; and they went further, for they used their native Aramaic tongue. Moreover, their entitlement to issue silver represents an unusual gradation of privilege[1]: for Augustus needed the advice of their Vizier when he sent an expedition to southern Arabia (25 B.C.).

Here, then, is the outermost layer of the empire's monetary system. Beyond the issuers of imperial, provincial and local currency, beyond the frontiers themselves, were dependent kings of many *nuances* of dependence, 'clients' of the emperor with ostensibly autonomous currencies. But even beyond the client-kings there was sometimes a penumbra of semi-client-kings, less dependent on Rome, tied to the emperors by economic rather than political bonds, comparable to the 'banana imperialism' of today. It has been suggested that Rome at one time intended the little Iberian monarchy to fulfil this role. But such ambiguous princelings are to be found across the frontiers in the West as well as in the East. For instance, Augustus possessed complex relations of this kind with Britain, beyond the north-western extremity of his empire. Administratively, Britain hung in the air. Julius Caesar had twice invaded it (55–54 B.C.), seeking military glory and the country's mineral wealth, which reports had exaggerated. But he did not achieve conquest; nor, despite

[1] The kingdom of the Crimean Bosphorus alone was allowed to issue gold (Pl. 32, no. 9).

the forecasts and boastings of court poets, did anyone else for almost a century. Meanwhile, there were a number of independent coining authorities in Britain. Foremost among them were two kingdoms ruled by Belgae, recent immigrants from across the Channel. One of these kingdoms comprised tribes in and around Sussex, Hampshire and Berkshire—the Regnenses (though this name may date only from the Roman conquest) and the Atrebates. Their first inscribed coins, perhaps issued in Sussex, show the name of Commius (Pl. 23, no. 7). He imitated the coin-types of northern France, for he had fled from that country when Caesar had defeated him there (52 B.C.).

His son Tincommius, however, borrowed the type of a horseman from Roman coinage (Pl. 23, no. 8); and this borrowing confirms other indications that he possessed close relations with the empire. Soon afterwards the geographer Strabo writes of the export to Rome of British corn, cattle, gold, silver, iron, hides, slaves and hunting hounds, exchanged for jewels, glass and other factory products. Augustus preferred the sound, unromantic economic method—with its lucrative customs dues—to imperialist adventures. He felt he could best influence Britain by financial bonds—and by the maintenance of a balance of power among the tribes. However, Tincommius was apparently regarded as a quisling by his compatriots, for he fled to Rome. But Augustus formed even closer relations with his successors Eppillus (Pl. 23, no. 9) and Verica (Pl. 23, no. 10). The former, coining at CALLE(*va*) (Silchester), calls himself King (REX), a Latin title which suggests that he regarded himself in some way as a client of Rome. Verica too displays a southward-looking design: the vine-leaf.

But these southern kingdoms were inferior in strength and ferocity to the more northern Belgic state of the Catuvellauni.

This tribe coined apparently first at Wheathampstead—until Caesar, overcoming an unexpected chariot-charge, sacked it— and then at VER(*ulamium*) (St Albans). The monarch who coined at Verulamium in Augustan times, Tasciovanus (Pl. 23, nos. 11 and 12), is unknown to history but proved by coin-finds to have ruled over a large territory—from the borders of the southern kingdom (and of a smaller Kentish state) to the Cherwell and the Nene or Welland. Coin-finds tell us a great deal about the boundaries of these British kingdoms: for instance, we are able to reconstruct from them that another tribe, the Dobuni, dwelt between the Kennet, the Cherwell and the Wye.

Caesar had forbidden the Catuvellauni to annex the Trinovantes (Essex). But the latter tribe were at least temporarily in the hands of Tasciovanus, for a few coins of this king bear the name of the Trinovantian centre CAM(*ulodunum*) (Lexden by Colchester). Lexden was the capital and mint of Tasciovanus' son and successor, the great Cunobelinus (*c*. A.D. 5–10 to 40–43)—Shakespeare's Cymbeline, the only king whose memory has survived in British tradition: he is celebrated by Geoffrey of Monmouth. Cunobelinus is REX (Pl. 23, no. 13); a Roman writer calls him 'Rex Britanniarum'. But this title no longer signifies client-status; it rather suggests indirect defiance of Rome. The ear of corn on his coins (Pl. 23, no. 14) recalls that the Trinovantes produced this leading export on a large scale. Cunobelinus controlled the Trinovantes, and all south-eastern Britain except the Iceni in East Anglia (Pl. 23, no. 16). He never made peace with Rome. But he maintained a vigorous cross-channel trade and he did not provoke war— unlike his son Caratacus (Pl. 23, no. 15), who thereby brought upon himself and his country defeat and annexation (A.D. 43–48).

Henceforward these tribes belonged to Rome. Yet another

of the border-lands had passed within the empire. Nevertheless, as Hadrian's Wall and the Antonine Wall demonstrate, the Romans never succeeded in annexing our whole island: thus our language and our culture to this day blend northern romanticism with Latin practicality. One of the most remarkable examples, however, of the practicality of the Romans is one which we, with our mass-media of communications, do not need to imitate, and so may find strange indeed: namely, their political exploitation of their coinage, of which something has been said in these pages.

NOTE ON ANCIENT AND MODERN BOOKS

A. Ancient Writers Mentioned in the Text

(i) *Greek*

STRABO, *c.* 63 B.C.–after A.D. 21, geographer.

APPIAN, second century A.D., historian of Rome.

DIO CHRYSOSTOM, *c.* A.D. 40–after 112, orator and historian.

PAUSANIAS, *c.* A.D. 150, traveller and philosopher.

GALEN, A.D. 129–*c.* 199, writer on philosophy and medicine.

DIO CASSIUS, third century, Roman history up to A.D. 229.

PHILOSTRATUS, *c.* A.D. 170–245, biographer (life of *Apollonius of Tyana*, etc.).

(ii) *Latin* [1]

VARRO, 116–27 B.C., encyclopaedic scholar.

JULIUS CAESAR, *Commentaries* (Gallic and Civil Wars).

AUGUSTUS, Acts (*Res Gestae: Monumentum Ancyranum*).

OVID, 43 B.C.–*c.* A.D. 17 (elegies and *Metamorphoses*).

SENECA THE YOUNGER, *c.* 5/4 B.C.–A.D. 65, philosopher, tragic dramatist, orator.

CALPURNIUS SICULUS, probably wrote *c.* A.D. 50–60, pastoral poet.

PLINY THE ELDER, A.D. 23–79, *Natural History*, etc.

MARTIAL, *c.* A.D. 40–104, epigrammatist.

TACITUS, *c.* A.D. 55–after 115, historian (*Annals; Histories; Agricola; Germania; Dialogue on Orators*).

SUETONIUS, *c.* A.D. 69–*c.* 140, biographer, etc. (*Lives of the Caesars*).

AURELIUS VICTOR, *c.* A.D. 360, biographer (*The Caesars*).

Historia Augusta (biographies), *c.* A.D. 350–363.

[1] Translations of *Caesar* (Gallic War), *Tacitus* (Annals, Agricola, Germania), and *Suetonius,* in Penguin Classics; of others (in large part)—except *Aurelius Victor*—in Loeb edition also.

B. Some Modern Books

BARROW, R. H., *The Romans*, Pelican Books, 1949.

CARY, M., and HAARHOFF, H. J., *Life and Thought in the Graeco-Roman World*, Methuen, 1940.

CHARLESWORTH, M. P., *The Roman Empire*, O.U.P., 1951.

GRANT, M., *Roman Imperial Money*, Nelson, 1954.

HEAD, B. V., *Historia Numorum*, Clarendon Press, 2nd ed., 1911.

HILL, G. F., *Historical Roman Coins*, Constable, 1909.

MATTINGLY, H., *Roman Coins*, Methuen, 2nd ed., 1960.

RICHMOND, I. A., *Roman Britain*, Pelican Books, 1955.

ROSE, H. J., *Ancient Roman Religion*, Hutchinson, 1948.

SELTMAN, C. T., *Greek Coins*, Methuen, 2nd ed., 1955.

SUTHERLAND, C. H. V., *Coinage in Roman Imperial Policy, 31 B.C.–A.D. 68*, Methuen, 1951.

SUTHERLAND, C. H. V., *Art in Coinage*, Batsford, 1955.

SYDENHAM, E. A., *Coinage of the Roman Republic*, Spink, 1952.

TOYNBEE, J. M. C., *Roman Medallions*, American Numismatic Society, 1944.

VERMEULE, C. C., *Some Notes on Ancient Dies and Coining Methods*, Spink, 1954.

WHEELER, R. E. M., *Rome Beyond the Imperial Frontiers*, Bell, 1954.

KEY TO PLATES: METALS

(N = gold, R = silver, R(B) = base silver, Æ = bronze, Æ(S) = silvered bronze, Æ* = bronze, perhaps with zinc or other admixture.)

Pl. 1, nos. 1–8 R; Pl. 2, nos. 1–7 R, no. 8 N, nos. 9–10 R; Pl. 3, no. 1 N, no. 2 Æ, no. 3 Æ(S), no. 4 R, no. 5 N, no. 6 Æ; Pl. 4, nos. 1–2 brass, no. 3 Æ, no. 4 Æ(S), nos. 5–7 N; Pl. 5, no. 1 R, nos. 2–3 copper, no. 4 gilt Æ*, no. 5 Æ, nos. 6–7 (?) Æ(S); Pl. 6, nos. 1–3 N, no. 4 Æ, nos. 5–8 R, no. 9 *N*, no. 10 *Æ*; Pl. 7, no. 1 brass, nos. 2–5 *Æ*, no. 6 *N*, no. 7 *Æ*, nos. 8–10 brass; Pl. 8, nos. 1–3 *N*, no. 4 brass, no. 5 copper, no. 6 *N*, no. 7 copper, no. 8 brass; Pl. 9, nos. 1–4 brass, no. 5 *N*, no. 6 Æ; Pl. 10, no. 1 *Æ*, no. 2 brass, no. 3 *Æ*, nos. 4–5 *Æ*(B), no. 6 brass, no. 7 *N*; Pl. 11, no. 1 brass, no. 2 *N*, no. 3 brass, nos. 4–5 *N*, no. 6 brass, nos. 7–9 *N*; Pl. 12, no. 1 brass, no. 2 *N*, no. 3 *Æ*, no. 4 Æ, nos. 5–6 copper, nos. 7–8 brass; Pl. 13, no. 1 Æ*, no. 2 *Æ*(B), no. 3 brass, no. 4 Æ, no. 5 Æ(S), no. 6 *N*, no. 7 *Æ*, nos. 8–10 *N*; Pl. 14, nos. 1–2 *Æ*, no. 3 *N*, nos. 4–7 *Æ*, no. 8 *N*, no. 9 copper, no. 10 brass, no. 11 *N*; Pl. 15, no. 1 *Æ*, nos. 2–5 brass, no. 6 Æ, no. 7 Æ* (two metals); Pl. 16, no. 1 *Æ*(B), nos. 2–3 *N*, no. 4 Æ(S), no. 5 *N*, no. 6 Æ(S), no. 7 gilt Æ* (two metals), no. 8 *N*; Pl. 17, nos. 1–2 *N*, no. 3 *Æ*, nos. 4–5 *N*, no. 6 Æ, nos. 7–8 *N*; Pl. 18, nos. 1–6 brass; Pl. 19, no. 1 *N*, nos. 2–4 brass, nos. 5–6 brass or Æ*, no. 7 Æ, no. 8 *Æ*; Pl. 20, no. 1 *N*, nos. 2–3 brass or Æ*, nos. 4–5 *Æ*(R), no. 6 Æ*, nos. 7–8 Æ(S), no. 9 *N*; Pl. 21, no. 1 *N*, nos. 2–4 Æ, nos. 5–6 Æ*, nos. 7–8 Æ(S), nos. 9–10 *N*; Pl. 22, nos. 1–2 *N*, no. 3 *Æ*(B), no. 4 *N*, no. 5 *Æ*(B), no. 6 Æ(S), nos. 7–9 Æ; Pl. 23, nos. 1–3 Æ(S), no. 4 *Æ*, nos. 5–8 *N*, no. 9 *Æ*, no. 10 *N*, nos. 11–12 *Æ*, no. 13 Æ, no. 14 *N*, no. 15 *Æ*, no. 16 *N*; Pl. 24 nos. 1–2 *Æ*, no. 3 Æ*, no. 4 *N*, no. 5 Æ(S), no. 6 *N*, no. 7 Æ(S), nos. 8–10 *N*; Pl. 25, no. 1 copper or Æ*, no. 2 *Æ*, no. 3 brass, no. 4 Æ, no. 5 Æ*, no. 6 brass, no. 7 *Æ*; Pl. 26, no. 1 *N*, no. 2 *Æ*, nos. 3–4 *N*, no. 5 Æ*, no. 6 *Æ*(B), no. 7 brass, no. 8 *Æ*, no. 9 *N*, no. 10 Æ; Pl. 27, no. 1 *N*, no. 2 brass, no. 3 *N*, no. 4 Æ* or copper, no. 5 *N*, no. 6 Æ(S), no. 7 *N*, no. 8 Æ(S), no. 9 *Æ*; Pl. 28, nos. 1–8 Æ; Pl. 29, no. 1 *Æ*, no. 2 brass, no. 3 *Æ*, nos. 4–6 Æ, no. 7 *N*, no. 8 Æ(S), no. 9 *Æ*, no. 10 *N*; Pl. 30, no. 1 Æ, no. 2 *Æ*, nos. 3–7 Æ; Pl. 31, nos. 1–7 Æ; Pl. 32, nos. 1–2 *Æ*, no. 3 copper, no. 4 *Æ*, no. 5 Æ, no. 6 *Æ*, nos. 7–8 Æ, no. 9 *N*, nos. 10–11 *Æ*.

INDEX

93

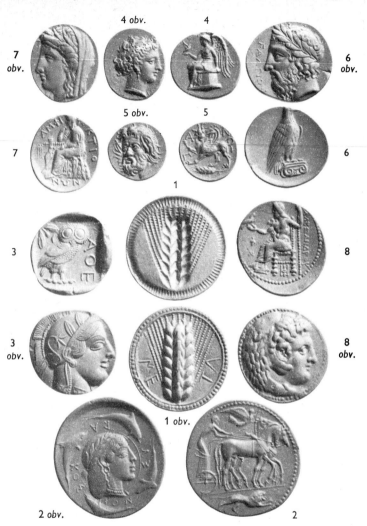

PLATE I. THE GREEKS (CH. I)

[1] Metapontum (south Italy), 530–510 B.C. [2] King Gelon of Syracuse, c. 479. [3] Athens, c. 440. [4] Terina (south-west Italy), c. 400; engraved by Euainetos. [5] Panticapaeum (Crimea), c. 380–360; satyr, griffin. [6] Olympia, c. 340; Zeus. [7] Delphi (under Alexander), c. 335; Demeter, Apollo. [8] Babylon, Alexander, c. 325; Heracles, Zeus.

PLATE 2. PORTRAITURE, 200–40 B.C. (CH. I)

[1] Antimachus of Bactria, *c.* 190 B.C., Poseidon. [2] Perseus of Macedonia, *c.* 175. [3] L. Brutus and Ahala, legendary liberators, *c.* 60. [4] Antius Restio, ancient tribune, *c.* 46; Hercules. [5] Pompey (posthumous), *c.* 46–45; Hispania welcomes his son. [6] Caesar, 44; Juno. [7] Brutus, 43–42; cap of liberty and daggers. [8] Antony and Octavian, 43. [9] Lepidus, *c.* 42. [10] Ahenobarbus, admiral, 41–40.

PLATE 3. ETERNAL ROME (CH. I AND III, § 2)

[1] Roman war goddess (Campania ?), *c.* 180 B.C.; Castor and Pollux.
[2] Gordian II, A.D. 238; Eternal Rome. [3] Maximinus II, 305–6; Genius
of the Roman People. [4] Eugenius (Lugdunum), 392–4; the City of Rome.
[5] Priscus Attalus (medallion), 414–16; Unconquerable Eternal Rome
(Invicta Roma Aeterna). [6] Ostrogothic kings of Italy, Theoderic etc.,
493–552; wolf and twins.

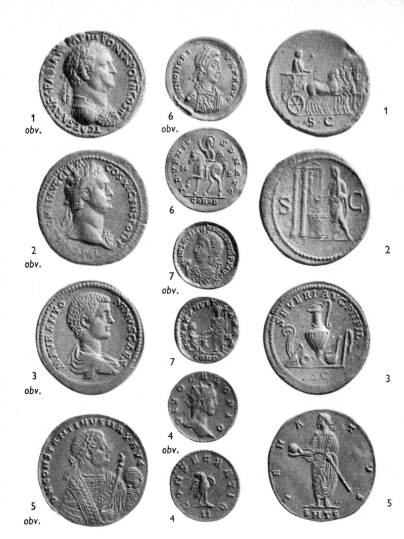

PLATE 4. IMPERIAL CEREMONIAL (CH. I)

[1] Titus (under Vespasian), A.D. 72; triumphal procession for conquest of Jews. [2] Domitian, 85; sacrifice to Minerva. [3] Caracalla (under Severus), 196–7; emblems of priesthoods. [4] Carus, deified (Lugdunum), 283. [5] Constantine (Thessalonica), c. 320; the senate personified. [6] Honorius (Mediolanum), 395–423; imperial visit. [7] Valentinian III, c. 455; public oath of loyalty extended from thirty to forty years.

PLATE 5. THE SACRED COINAGE (CH. I)

[1] T. Carisius, 45 B.C.; coining implements. [2] Domitian, A.D. 86; imperial coinage personified. [3] Commodus, 190; Apollo patron of the mint. [4 and 5] Medallions of Probus (with Sun), 276–82, and Maximian (as Hercules), 286–310, the three Monetae (gold, silver, bronze). [6 and 7] Diocletian, 284–305; Sacra Moneta, and Moneta with Jupiter and Hercules (medallion).

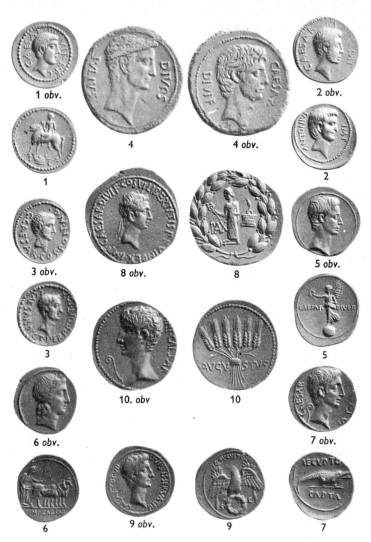

PLATE 6. AUGUSTUS AS AVENGER AND LIBERATOR (CH. II, I)

[1] North Italy, 41 B.C.; as Triumvir: his equestrian statue. [2] Gaul, 39; with Antony. [3] Gaul, 40–36; with Caesar, 'Perpetual Dictator'. [4] Same; 'son of the divine Julius'. [5] East, 31–29; for victory at Actium. [6] East, 29–28; settlement of ex-soldiers. [7] East, 28; conquest of Egypt. [8] East, 28; Liberator, Pax. [9] West, 27; Saviour, Augustus. [10] Chios, 27–20.

PLATE 7. AUGUSTUS AS RULER AND GOD (CH. II, 1)

[1] Rome, 20–18 B.C.; laurels, oak-wreath for saving citizens' lives.
[2] Gaul, *c.* 19; Roman standards recovered from Parthians. [3] Spain,
c. 18–17; 'shield of the virtues' conferred on Augustus. [4] Gaul, 19–16;
Mars the Avenger. [5] Rome, *c.* 13–12; with Agrippa. [6] Gaul, 10–9;
Augustus' patron Apollo. [7] Lugdunum, A.D. 13–14; Pater Patriae,
Pontifex Maximus. [8 and 9] Augustus deified (Tiberius). [10] The same
(Titus, 'restored' coin).

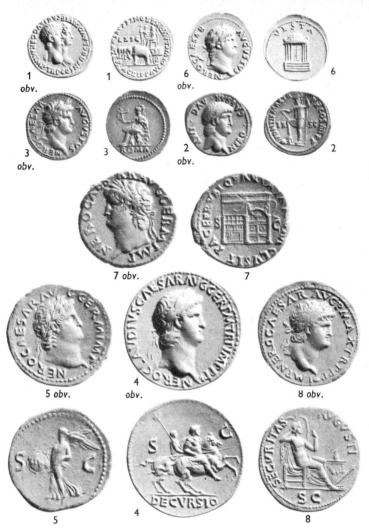

PLATE 8. NERO AS STATESMAN (CH. II, 2)

[1] With his mother Agrippina, A.D. 54. [2] Roman Courage (Virtus), 63–4.
[3] Roma, 64–8. [4] Emperor riding on manoeuvres (Decursio), 64–6.
[5] Victory (very large issue). [6] Temple of Vesta; rebuilt after Great Fire,
64 (types reproduced from Pl. 7, 8 and 9, in honour of Augustus who had
died fifty years earlier). [7] Temple of Janus, closed when empire is at
peace. [8] Security of emperor (Lugdunum), c. 66–8.

PLATE 9. NERO AS BENEFACTOR (CH. II, 2)

[1] Apollo, patron of culture (cf. Pl. 7, 6), A.D. 64–6. [2] Claudius' harbour at Ostia (opened by Nero). [3] Ceres and Annona, goddesses of corn-supply. [4] Provision market (Macellum Augusti), rebuilt after fire. [5] Imperial Concord. [6] 'Contorniate', prize or memento of public games, c. 390; Nero, games in Circus Maximus.

PLATE 10. IMPERIAL WOMEN, 40 B.C.–A.D. 83 (CH. II, 3)

[1] Cleopatra VII of Egypt (Ascalon). [2] Agrippina the elder, m. Germanicus, A.D. 37–9 (posthumous). [3] Agrippina the younger (Antioch), 54–9; with her son Nero. [4] Nero with his first wife Octavia (Alexandria), 56–7. [5] With his second wife Poppaea, 64–5. [6 and 7] Domitian's wife Domitia, c. 81–3; with their dead child.

PLATE II. IMPERIAL WOMEN, A.D. 79–161 (CH. II, 3)

[1 and 2] Julia daughter of Titus; Vesta (A.D. 79–81), Juno's peacock (86–91). [3 to 5] Trajan's sister Marciana (deified, 114–17), his niece Matidia, his wife Plotina (117–18). [6] Hadrian's wife Sabina, 128 37. [7] Faustina the elder, wife of Antoninus, d. 141 (deified); orphan's home. [8 and 9] Faustina the younger, wife of Aurelius, 145–61; dove of Concord, Venus.

PLATE 12. IMPERIAL WOMEN, A.D. 161–235 (CH. II, 3)

[1] Lucilla, wife of L. Verus, A.D. 164–9; Fecunditas. [2] Didia Clara, daughter of Didius Julianus, 193; Hilaritas (Joyfulness). [3] J. Domna, 211–17; Moon in chariot. [4] Elagabalus' grandmother J. Maesa, 218–22. [5 and 6] His mother J. Soaemias; Venus Caelestis, Juno. [7 and 8] His first two wives, J. Paula and Aquilia Severa. [9] Orbiana, wife of Severus Alexander, 225–7.

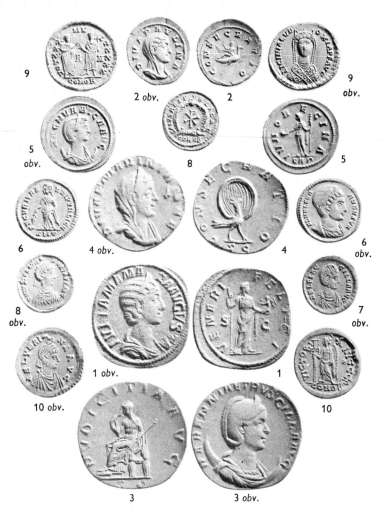

PLATE 13. IMPERIAL WOMEN, A.D. 222–474 (CH. II, 3)

[1] Sev. Alexander's mother J. Mamaea, A.D. 222–35. [2] Paulina, m.
Maximinus I, 235–8 (deified). [3] Etruscilla, m. Decius, 249–51; Pudicitia
(Modesty). [4] Mariniana, m. Valerian, 253–7 (deified). [5] Magnia
Urbica, m. Carinus, 282–3; Juno. [6] Constantine's mother Helena
(Ticinum), c. 324. [7] Flacilla, m. Theodosius I (Constantinople), 383–8.
[8 and 9] Valentinian III's sister Honoria and wife Eudoxia, c. 430–7.
[10] Verina, m. Leo I (Constantinople), 457–74.

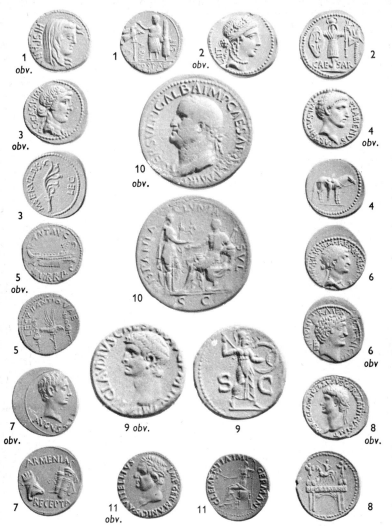

PLATE 14. WAR, 80 B.C.–A.D. 69 (CH. III, I)

[1] A. Postumius Albinus, *c.* 79 B.C.; Hispania with hair dishevelled (revolt of Sertorius). [2] Caesar (Gaul), *c.* 50, after defeat of Vercingetorix. [3] Cassius (Sardes), 42, before Philippi; ship's stern. [4] Q. Labienus, renegade (Cilicia), 40–39. [5] Antony. [6] with Cleopatra, 33–31. [7] Augustus, Armenia recovered, 20–19. [8 and 9] Claudius, A.D. 41–2; his father Nero Drusus (on the 50th anniversary of his death) and Minerva. [10] Galba, 68–9; Hispania. [11] Vitellius (Spain), 69; Clemency.

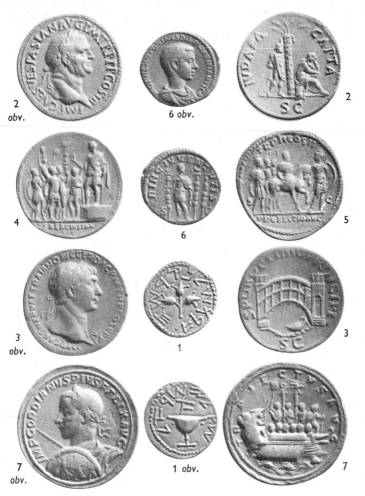

PLATE 15. WAR, A.D. 66–244 (CH. III, 1)

[1] Jews in revolt, A.D. 66; chalice and pomegranates. [2] Vespasian, 71;
Jewish revolt suppressed. [3] Trajan, c. 104–6; Danube bridge, for Dacian
campaigns. [4] Hadrian, c. 135; the army in Spain. [5] L. Verus, 162;
departure to fight Parthia. [6] Diadumenian, heir to Macrinus, 217–18;
Prince of Youth. [7] Gordian III (medallion), 242; crossing into Asia to
fight Persians.

PLATE 16. WAR, A.D. 253–361 (CH. III, I)

[1] Aemilian, A.D. 253; Mars the peace-bringer. [2] Victorinus, ruler in western provinces, 268–70; Victory. [3] Tetricus, his successor, 270–3 (conquered by Aurelian). [4] Zenobia, queen of Palmyra, 270–1 (Alexandria) (conquered by Aurelian). [5] Aurelian (Siscia), 270–3. [6] Probus, 281. [7] Numerian (medallion), 283; address to troops fighting Persians. [8] Constantius II (medallion, Nicomedia), in full dress, 337–61; Constantinopolis.

PLATE 17. WAR, A.D. 337–476 (CH. III, I)

[1] Constans (medallion, Aquileia), *c.* A.D. 347.   [2] Decentius, brother of Magnentius, 350–3; Victory and Liberty.   [3] Valens (medallion, Treveri), 367–75; triumph over barbarians.   [4] Gratian, 375–8.   [5] Theodosius I (Siscia), 378–83; the army's courage.   [6] Arcadius (Thessalonica), 383–8; Roman glory.   [7] Johannes (Ravenna), 423–5.   [8] Libius Severus, 461–5. [9] Romulus Augustulus, last western emperor, 475–6.

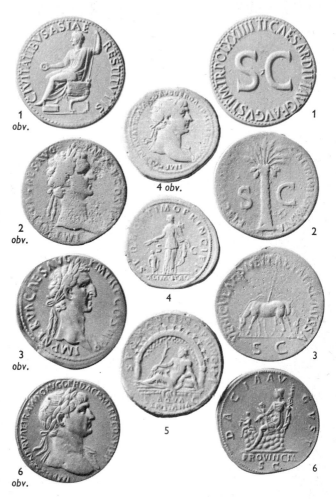

PLATE 18. RESTORATION AND REFORM, A.D. 14–117 (CH. III, 2)

[1] Tiberius, A.D. 22–3; the cities of Asia helped after earthquakes.
[2] Nerva, 96; Jewish tax regulated. [3] Nerva, 97; imperial post abolished.
[4–6] Trajan; 107–11, aid to orphans and farmers (Alimenta Italiae);
c. 112–14, improved Roman water supply (Aqua Traiana); Dacia re-
habilitated.

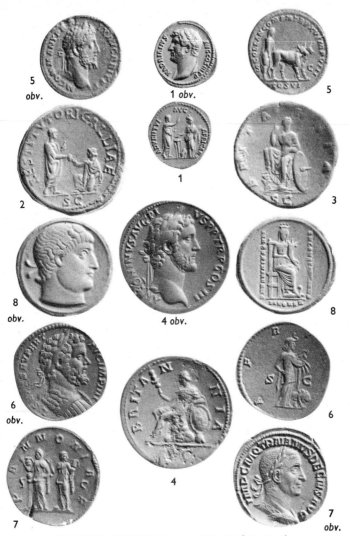

PLATE 19. THE EMPIRE, A.D. 117–337 (CH. III, 2)

Hadrian's three series in honour of provincial territories, *c.* A.D. 134:
[1] Visit to Africa. [2] Gallia restored. [3] Britannia. [4] Antoninus
Pius, 143–4; Britannia (cf. British pennies). [5] Commodus, 190; Hercules
ploughs furrow of Rome refounded. [6] Severus, 194–5; his homeland
Africa. [7] Decius, 249–51; his homeland, the two Pannonias. [8] Constantine, *c.* 330 (medallion); foundation of Constantinopolis as new
capital.

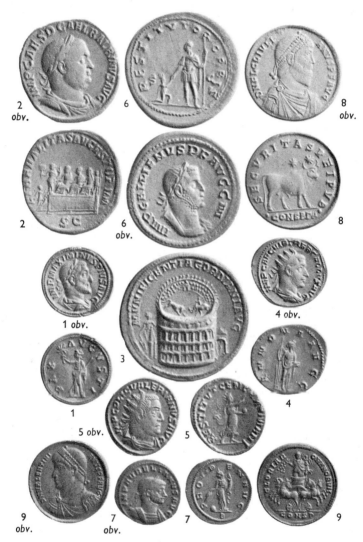

PLATE 20. IMPERIAL BENEVOLENCE, A.D. 235–375 (CH. III, 2)

[1] Maximinus I the Thracian, A.D. 235–6; Peace. [2] Balbinus, 238; food-distribution. [3] Gordian III (medallion), 244; Colosseum. [4] Gallus, 251–3; corn-supply. [5 and 6] Valerian (Antioch), 253–4, and Gallienus, 257–9; restorers of the world. [7] Aurelian, 270–5; forethought of emperor. [8] Julian the Apostate (Constantinople), 362–3; leader of the herd. [9] Valentinian I (Constantinople), 364–7; largess.

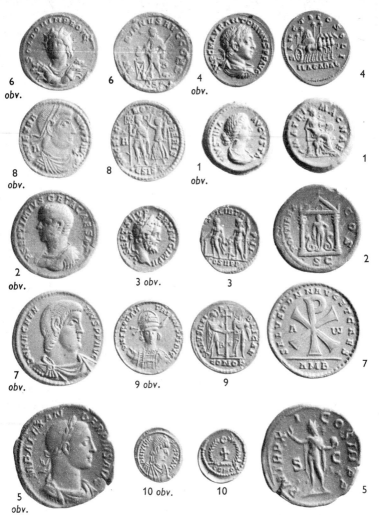

PLATE 21. UN-ROMAN DEITIES, A.D. 161–476 (CH. III, 2)

[1] Faustina the younger, A.D. 169–75; the Great Mother (Cybele).
[2] Geta, 203; Aesculapius. [3 and 4] The native gods of Severus, 194, and
Elagabalus, 218–19. [5] Sev. Alexander, 232. [6] Aurelian (Serdica), 271;
the Sun. [7] Magnentius (Ambiani), c. 350; Christogram. [8] Vetranio
(Siscia), 350; Constantine's vision. [9] Anthemius (Ravenna), 467–72.
[10] Julius Nepos, 474–5; the Cross.

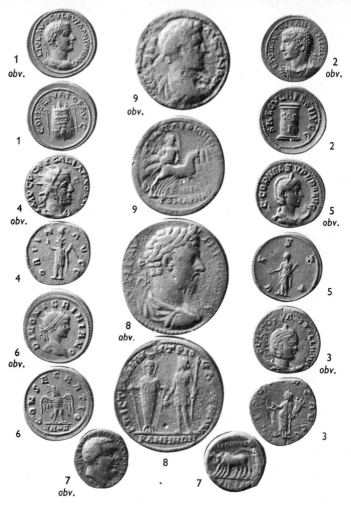

PLATE 22. UNKNOWN PEOPLE AND PLACES (CH. IV, I)

[1 and 2] Uranius Antoninus (Emesa), A.D. 253–4. [3 and 4] Dryantilla and Regalian (Carnuntum), 259–60; Equity, Sun. [5] Cornelia Supera, m. Aemilian, 253; Vesta. [6] Nigrinian, son of Carinus, 284–5 (deified). [7] M. Rutilus (Lystra ?), 44–43 B.C., priest ploughing çolony's furrow. [8] M. Aurelius (Came), A.D. 161–80; Dionysus and archaic statue. [9] Commodus (Tomara), 176–92; Rape of Persephone.

PLATE 23. ROMAN AND PRE-ROMAN BRITAIN (CH. IV, 2 AND V, 2)

[1 and 2] Carausius, A.D. 288–93 (?Clausentum = Bitterne); co-emperors, Secular Games. [3] (London) Maximian. [4] Carausius, Wolf and twins. [5] Allectus, 293–6; Sun. [6] Magnus Maximus (London), 383–8—Pre-Conquest: [7] Commius (Atrebates). [8] Tincommius. [9] Eppillus (Calleva = Silchester). [10] Verica. [11, 12] Tasciovanus (Catuvellauni). [13, 14] Cunobelinus (Camulodunum = Colchester). [15] Caratacus. [16] The Iceni.

PLATE 24. TWO ARTISTIC THEMES: BUILDINGS AND FRONTAL
PORTRAITS (CH. IV, 2)

[1] M. Lepidus, *c.* 66 B.C.; Basilica Aemilia. [2] Claudius (Ephesus),
c. A.D. 41–2; t. Diana. [3 and 4] bicentenaries of 'accession' and death of
Augustus, Antoninus Pius, 158–9; t. Augustus and Livia: and Caracalla,
214; t. Vesta. [5] Romulus son of Maxentius, *c.* 310 (deified); his t. —.
[6] Postumus (Cologne), 259–68; Indulgence. [7] Carausius (Clausentum),
288–93; Well-being (Salus). [8] Maxentius (Ostia), *c.* 308. [9] Licinius
junior (Nicomedia), *c.* 312. [10] Olybrius, 472.

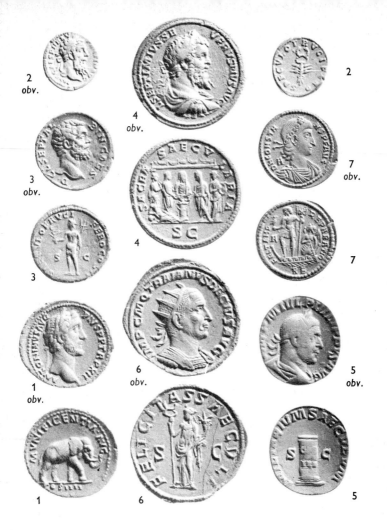

PLATE 25. THE GOLDEN AGE (CH. IV, 2)

[1] Antoninus Pius, A.D. 148; munificence on 900th anniversary of Rome.
[2] Pertinax, 193; and [3] Clodius Albinus, 194–6; the Fruitful Age
(Saeculum Frugiferum). [4 and 5] Secular Games of Severus, 204, and
Philip sen., 248 (millenary: Miliarium Saeculum). [6] Decius, 249–51;
Happiness of the Age. [7] Constans, 348 (1100th anniversary?), Happy
Times Recovered.

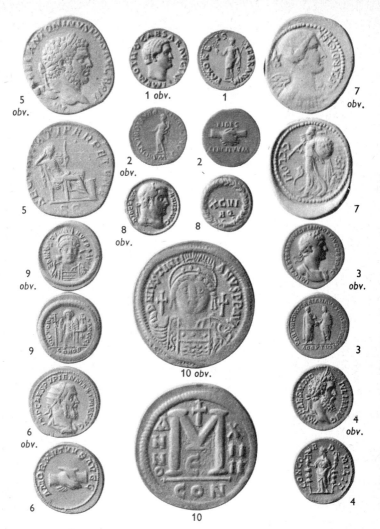

PLATE 26. POLITICAL FICTIONS AND ECONOMIC FACTS (CH. IV, 2)

[1] Otho, A.D. 69; World Peace. [2] Civil War, 69–70; Concord, Loyalty.
[3] Hadrian, 117; his 'adoption'. [4] Didius Julianus, 193; concord.
[5] Caracalla, 210–11; perpetual security. [6] Pupienus, 238; co-emperors'
mutual affection.—[7] Caesar (Mediolanum?), 45 B.C.; Minerva (brass).
[8] Diocletian (Aquileia), c. A.D. 296; 1/96 pound. [9 and 10] Justin I,
518–27, Justinian I, 540–1; 10th, 5th mint sections (I, E).

PLATE 27. DEVOTION TO THE PAST (CH. IV, 2)

[1] Nero Drusus (posthumous, A.D. 41–2) and [2] Domitian (85); German shields—[2] on centenary of Nero Drusus's march to the Danube. [3] Antoninus Pius, c. 140; Aeneas leaving Troy. [4] M. Aurelius (medallion), 168; Jupiter protecting the co-emperors. [5] Commodus, 186–7; supreme Jupiter. [6] Tacitus, 275–6; Well-being (Salus). [7] Diocletian (Nicomedia), 284–305; Jupiter and eagle. [8] Galerius, c. 308; emperor's Genius. [9] Gratian (Lugdunum), 378–83; Roman courage.

PLATE 28. CITIZEN SETTLEMENTS. PROVINCIAL ASSEMBLIES
(CH. V, I)

[1] Augustus and Agrippa (Nemausus, Gaul), *c.* 14–12 B.C. (counter-marked); crocodile. [2] Varus (Achulla, Africa), *c.* 7–6 B.C. [3] Caligula (Apamea, Bithynia), his sisters (Drusilla deified). [4] Caligula (Patrae), A.D. 37, thanked for leave to coin. [5] Sinope, 1st cent. A.D. (*Colonia Iulia Felix*); Diogenes. [6] Caracalla (Comama, Pisidia), 211–17; two cult-images.—[7] Hadrian (Bithynia), 117–38. [8] Severus (Cyprus), 193–211; t. Aphrodite, Paphos (in perspective).

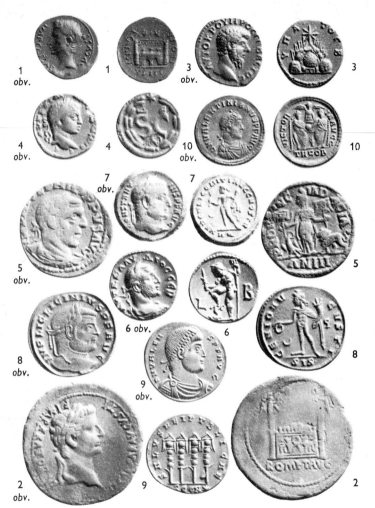

PLATE 29. IMPERIAL AND PROVINCIAL MINTS (CH. V, I)

[1] Augustus (view of Emerita, Spain), 25–22 B.C., and [2] (Lugdunum, head of Tiberius), A.D. 13–14. [3] L. Verus (Caesarea, Cappadocia), 161–6; mt. Argaeus. [4] Elagabalus (Antioch), 218–22. [5] Philip sen. (Dacia personified), 248–9; [6] Claudius Gothicus (Alexandria), 269–70; Poseidon. [7] Constantius I (Aquileia), 305–6; Hercules. [8] Licinius sen. (Siscia), *c.* 308; Genius. [9] Valens (Arelate), 364–7. [10] Valentinian II (Thessalonica), 378–83.

PLATE 30. CITY-MINTS (CH. V, I)

[1] Castulo, Spain, c. 35–25 B.C.; names of town-officials. [2] Caligula (Hierapytna, Crete), A.D. 37–41; with deified Augustus. [3] Rhodes ('didrachm'), early principate; Sun, Nike. [4] Antinous (Ancyra), 134–8; Mên. [5] Commodus and Crispina (Byzantium), 177–80; helmet. [6] Plautilla, wife of Caracalla (Aegira, Peloponnese), 202–5; Zeus. [7] Julia Domna (Damascus), 211–17; city-goddess.

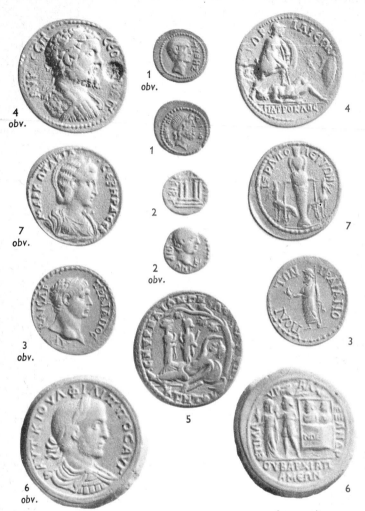

PLATE 31. CITY-MINTS: PROVINCE OF ASIA (CH. V, 1)

[1] Local notable Pythes (Laodicea), time of Augustus; head of Laodicean people. [2] Governor Q. Veranius (Cibyra), *c*. A.D. 43–5. [3] Trajan (new foundation Trajanopolis), 98–117; Zeus. [4] Severus (Ilium), 193–211; Hector and Patroclus. [5] Philip sen. (Smyrna), 244–9; Alexander's vision of two Nemeses. [6] Philip sen. (Apamea, Phrygia); Noah's ark. [7] His wife Otacilia Severa (Hierapolis); Artemis.

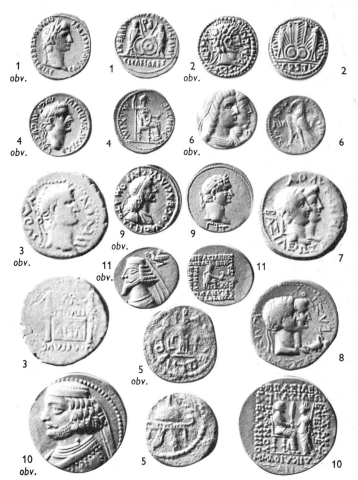

PLATE 32. BEYOND THE FRONTIERS (CH. V, 2)

[1] Augustus, 2 B.C.–A.D. 14; his grandsons. [2] barbarous imitation.
[3] barbarous imitation (cf. Pl. 29, 2). [4] Tiberius, A.D. 14–37; Peace-
Justice.—[5] Herod (Jerusalem), 43–44 B.C.; helmet, tripod. [6] Obodas III
(Nabataea), A.D. 30–9. [7, 8] Rhoemetalces I (Thrace), 11 B.C.–A.D. 12;
Augustus and Livia. [9] Sauromates I (Crimean Bosphorus), A.D. 96;
Domitian. [10] Orodes II (Parthia), 57–37 B.C., greeted by Seleucia-on-
Tigris. [11] Phraates IV, 37–2; warrior.